Psalms 149:3 Let them praise his name in the dance. (kjv)

DANCE MINISTRY 101
GENESIS TO REVELATION

DR. DAPHNE R. SNOWDEN

"Life is perfect
when I minister
through dance!"

~ drs

Table Of Content

1. Spiritual Growth
2. Tithes And Tithing
3. Prayer And Fasting
4. Colors In Ministry
5. Garments
6. Props In Ministry
7. Mentorship
8. Fellowship
9. Fundraising
10. Life-Long Learner
11. Dance Practice

1. Song Selction Aligned With Scripture
2. Vision For The Dance
3. Dance Technique
4. Choreography

1. Succession Planning
2. Strategic Planning

My name is Dr. Daphne Renee Snowden. I have a diverse portfolio of professional and personal experiences that make me the women that I am today. I am a Christian, liturgical dancer, entrepreneur, educator, ministry leader, grant writer, college professor, global presenter, facilitator, veteran, community advocate, succession planning consultant, nutrition and fitness coach, Yoga and Zumba instructor. I honor my civic duty to give back to my community, where I lead and serve on multiple church ministries and community organizations. I am the proud mother of one son, Christopher Jamal Snowden, and proud grandmother of one grandson Christopher Jamal Snowden Jr. "Baby CJ", both of whom I love dearly. "All my love all my life!" I am a proud member of Delta Sigma Theta Sorority, Incorporated. My core values include Christian principles, honesty, respect, and integrity. I maintain a strong commitment to church, family, education, sisterhood, entrepreneurship, fitness, dance, and continued personal and professional growth.

I have a diverse educational background that includes a Doctor of Education from Morgan State University, both Master and Bachelor of Science degrees in Criminal Justice from Coppin State University. I am also a Professional Life Coach, Happiness Coach, Life Purpose Coach, Goal Success Coach, Master Coach, Fitness Coach, Health and Nutrition Coach.

I have a passion for all types of dancing. I serve and minister with Shapely Fitness Liturgical Dance Ensemble, the Women of Worship at the Faith United Baptist Church, previously served with the : Maryland Academy of Dance, Ministry Ensemble, Nehemiah House Dance Ministry, Youth Dance Ministry Leader and briefly practiced with Divine Purpose Dance Ensemble. I am a certified Yoga and Zumba Dance Instructor. Where, I offer fitness dance classes and life coaching services through Shapely Fitness LLC, where I am the Founder and lead instructor.

Over the years, I have served on various dance ministries under multiple leaders. I have ministered under exceptional dance ministry leaders and other leaders that could benefit from a leadership development program or *"THIS BOOK".* These diverse experiences led me to writing this book. Dance ministries have so much to offer when managed by trained leaders that recognize the distinct differences between a dance ministry and a dance class. Successful dance ministry leaders develop Godly dancers that use the dance worship experience to usher in the Holy Spirit in preparation for the preached word used to lead souls to Christ!

Dr. Daphne Snowden, Founder
Shapely Fitness LLC
shapelyfitness@yahoo.com
http://daphnsnowden.zumba.com

"A Christian Committed to a Christian-Fitness Dance Platform!"

~ drs

CHAPTER I.

Purpose

Dr. Daphne Snowden
Shapely Fitness, Gospel Fitness & Liturgical Dance
Faith United Baptist Church, Women of Worship
Maryland Academy of Dance, Ministry Ensemble (Former)
Nehemiah House Ministries, Dance Ministry
John Wesley United Methodist Church, Youth Dance Ministry Leader

1. This journal is designed to groom dance ministry leaders by teaching them how to start, grow, and develop a successfully anointed dance ministry. Students will learn how to minister through dance and how to set the atmosphere through praise and worship.

2. This journal will catapult each dance ministry to the next level through scripture-based lectures and dance movement exercises.

3. This journal is for anyone who is interested in growing as a ministry dancer, ministry dance leader or in developing a dance ministry.

The purpose of this book is to offer a scripture foundation for dance ministry leaders and participants about the difference between dance ministry and dance class. Although both have great qualities, there are distinct differences that must be recognized specifically when leading or participating in a dance ministry. Dance Ministry Leaders must clearly understand the responsibilities of leading a dance ministry because it is so much more than choreography and dancing. A Dance Ministry Leader must build Godly dancers, that are spiritually, mentally, and physically prepared to embrace a worship experience through dance.

This book is designed to serve as a management tool for dance ministry leaders, providing a framework that: **(1)** provides a scriptural overview of dance, **(2)** outlines the purpose of the dance ministry community, **(3)** outlines the characteristics of a successful dance ministry, **(4)** describes the responsibilities of a dance ministry leader, and (5) provides a framework to plan for the future of dance ministries.

After reading this book and applying the principles, dance ministry leaders will be positioned to: (1) lead a Godly dance ministry that self-markets new participants, (2) lead a Godly ministry that encourages and develops Godly dancers that are spiritually, mentally, and physically prepared, (3) lead a Godly dance ministry that establishes life-long friendships, and (4) most importantly, lead a Godly Dance Ministry that brings souls to Christ through dance. This book will frame the dance ministry legacy, with succession planning strategies that ensure the ministry survives!

"When your heart is heavy speak to God
through the dance!"

Let's talk about your dance ministry!

(1) What is the name of your Dance Ministry? _____

(2) What is your role on the dance ministry? ( ) Leader ( ) Dancer
If you are the leader, what qualifies you to serve as the dance ministry leader?

_____

_____

_____

_____

_____

(3) Dance Ministry Schedule:
     a)Prayer Time: _____

     b)Bible Study: _____

(4) What is the purpose or mission of the dance ministry?

_____

_____

_____

_____

_____

_____

(5) Is the dance ministry fulfilling its purpose? ( ) Yes ( ) No

Explain your response: _____

_____

_____

_____

_____

_____

(6) What is unique (if anything) about the dance ministry?

_____

_____

_____

_____

(7) How many dancers serve on the dance ministry? _____

(8) When does the dance ministry practice? ————————————

(9) How long is a normal dance practice? ————————————

(10) When is the dance ministry scheduled to minister? ————————

(11) When and where does the dance ministry fellowship? ————————

————————————————————————————————

————————————————————————————————

(12) How often does the dance ministry fellowship? ————————

————————————————————————————————

(13) What unique qualities or contributions do "each" dancer bring to the ministry, list 1-2 qualities for each dancer (list each dancer by name). Examples of unique qualities or contributions (may include but not limited to): choreographer, flagger, wardrobe and costumes, minister of prayer, events planner, singer, organizer, timekeeper, fitness, counselor, note taker, fundraiser, seamstress, gymnast, model, stepper, etc.

a. ————————————————————————————

b. ————————————————————————————

c. ————————————————————————————

d. ————————————————————————————

e. ————————————————————————————

f. ————————————————————————————

g. ————————————————————————————

h. ————————————————————————————

i. ————————————————————————————

(14) Were you able to identify a quality for each dancer: ( ) Yes, Excellent! ( ) No. List by name each dancer and create an individual plan to get to know each dancer listed.

a. ————————————————————————————

b. ————————————————————————————

c. ————————————————————————————

d. ————————————————————————————

e. ————————————————————————————

f. _____

g. _____

h. _____

(15) What measures will you implement to (a) ensure that you always recognize the uniqueness of each dancer? (b) How will you ensure that you acknowledge, utilize, and further develop each dancer's unique contributions to the ministry.

_____

_____

_____

_____

_____

(16) If you walked away today from the dance ministry, would the ministry be able to successfully continue to fulfill its mission and purpose? ( ) Yes ( ) No If "Yes" how? What measures have you implemented to ensure the continuation of the dance ministry?

a. _____

b. _____

c. _____

d. _____

e. _____

f. _____

g. _____

h. _____

i. _____

j. _____

If you answered No. No worries you are on the right track, by reading this book. This book is designed to outline a platform for all dance ministry leaders to ensure that the "ministry never dies".

"Dancer's shepherd in the Holy Spirt into the worship experience!"

~ drs

CHAPTER II.

Scripture Foundation for Dance

Worship is the foundation for dance in the bible because the bible commands that we worship God and dance is a form of worship *"WORSHIP THROUGH DANCE"*.

• Psalm 29:2 Give unto the Lord the glory due unto his name; worship the Lord in the beauty of holiness.
• Psalm 45:11 So shall the king greatly desire thy beauty: for he is thy Lord; and worship thou him.
• Psalm 95:6 O come, let us worship and bow down: let us kneel before the Lord our maker.
• Psalm 96:9 O worship the Lord in the beauty of holiness: fear before him, all the earth.
• Psalm 99:5 Exalt ye the Lord our God, and worship at his footstool; for he is holy. *(KJV)*

DANCERS WORSHIP because worship creates an atmosphere of truth that allows God's people to feel spiritually free.

• John 4:23 But the hour cometh, and now is, when the true worshippers shall worship the Father in spirit and in truth: for the Father seeketh such to worship him.
• John 4:24 God is a Spirit: and they that worship him must worship him in spirit and in truth.
• 1 Corinthians 14:25 And thus are the secrets of his heart made manifest; and so, falling down on his face he will worship God, and report that God is in you of a truth. *(KJV)*

It should be noted that the Bible does not give specific instructions on dancing; however, scriptures can be used to develop biblical principles to build dance ministry standards that govern Godly dance ministries. **Exodus 15:20** expresses that dancing was used to celebrate the victory of God's power. **2 Samuel 6:12-16** "danced before the Lord" to celebrate the Ark of the Covenant being brought back to Jerusalem. **Ecclesiastes 3:4** speaks to the appropriate time to dance. **Psalm 149:3** and **Psalms 150:4**, both scriptures reference that dancers can praise and worship God through dance. **Psalm 149:3** Let them praise His name with dancing and make music to him with tambourine and harp. **Psalms 150:4** Praise him with the timbrel and dance.

Old Testament

1. **Exodus 15:20** Then Miriam the prophetess, the sister of Aaron, took a tambourine in her hand, and all the women went out after her with tambourines and dancing.

2. **Exodus 32:19** And it came to pass, as soon as he came nigh unto the camp, that he saw the calf, and the dancing: and Moses' anger waxed hot, and he cast the tables out of his hands, and brake them beneath the mount.

3. **Judges 11:34** Then Jephthah came to his home at Mizpah. And behold, his daughter came out to meet him with tambourines and with dances. She was his only child; besides her he had neither son nor daughter.

4. **1 Samuel 18:6** As they were coming home, when David returned from striking down the Philistine, the women came out of all the cities of Israel, singing and dancing, to meet King Saul, with tambourines, with songs of joy, and with musical instruments.

5. **1 Samuel 21:11** And the servants of Achish said to him, "Is not this David the king of the land? Did they not sing to one another of him in dances, 'Saul has struck down his thousands, and David his ten thousands'?"

6. **1 Samuel 29:5** Is not this David, of whom they sing to one another in dances, 'Saul has struck down his thousands, and David his ten thousands'?"

7. **1 Samuel 30:16** And when he had taken him down, behold, they were spread abroad over all the land, eating and drinking and dancing, because of all the great spoil they had taken from the land of the Philistines and from the land of Judah.

8. **2 Samuel 6:14** And David danced before the Lord with all his might. And David was wearing a linen ephod.

9. **2 Samuel 6:16** As the ark of the Lord came into the city of David, Michal the daughter of Saul looked out of the window and saw King David leaping and dancing before the Lord, and she despised him in her heart.

10. **1 Chronicles 15:29** And as the ark of the covenant of the Lord came to the city of David, Michal the daughter of Saul looked out of the window and saw King David dancing and rejoicing, and she despised him in her heart.

11. **Job 21:11** They send out their little boys like a flock, and their children dance.

12. **Psalm 30:11** You have turned for me my mourning into dancing; you have loosed my sackcloth and clothed me with gladness.

13. **Psalm 149:3** Let them praise his name with dancing, making melody to him with tambourine and lyre!

14. **Psalm 150:4** Praise him with tambourine and dance; praise him with strings and pipe!

15. **Ecclesiastes 3:4** A time to weep, and a time to laugh; a time to mourn, and a time to dance.

16. **Song of Solomon 6:13** Return, return, O Shulammite, return, return, that we may look upon you. Why should you look upon the Shulammite, as upon a dance before two armies?

17. **Jeremiah 31:4** Again I will build you, and you shall be built, O virgin Israel! Again you shall adorn yourself with tambourines and shall go forth in the dance of the merrymakers.

18. **Jeremiah 31:13** Then shall the young women rejoice in the dance, and the young men and the old shall be merry. I will turn their mourning into joy; I will comfort them, and give them gladness for sorrow.

19. **Lamentations 5:15** The joy of our hearts has ceased; our dancing has been turned to mourning.

New Testament

20. **Matthew 14:6-8** But when Herod's birthday came, the daughter of Herodias danced before the company and pleased Herod, so that he promised with an oath to give her whatever she might ask. Prompted by her mother, she said, "Give me the head of John the Baptist here on a platter."

21. **Mark 6:22** For when Herodias's daughter came in and danced, she pleased Herod and his guests. And the king said to the girl, "Ask me for whatever you wish, and I will give it to you."

22. **Luke 7:32** They are like children sitting in the marketplace and calling to one another, We played the flute for you, and you did not dance; we sang a dirge, and you did not weep.

23. **Luke 15:25** "Now his older son was in the field, and as he came and drew near to the house, he heard music and dancing.

The Bible acknowledges dancing as a form of worship.
Dancers must ensure that the style of dance does not tempt self or others in a sinful manner; but that the dance movements honor and glorify God.
(https://www.gotquestions.org/Christian-dance.html)

Reflection

(1) Why do you think churches today include dance as a part of the worship experience?

_____

_____

_____

_____

_____

(2) Have you shared with the dance ministry members how dance or dancing is referenced in the bible? (   ) Yes (   ) No
If yes, in what context?

_____

_____

_____

What scripture?

_____

_____

What was the outcome?

_____

_____

(3) If No. How will you use bible scriptures that reference dance and dancing to educate the dance ministry members?

_____

_____

_____

_____

"Dancing is referenced in the Bible and is used throughout the
Old Testament as a means of worship and
praise to God"

~ Unknown

CHAPTER III

Introduction To Liturigical Dance

The word liturgical is used to describe a public religious ceremony or ritual. The liturgical dance ministry is a public form of physical praise and worship used to connect and convey a divine message that glorifies and exalts God through the art of dance. In **Psalms 150:4** the Bible reads, "praise him with timbrel and dancing, praise him with the strings and pipe". This demonstrates that God has ordained dance as a physical expression of acknowledging him in worship. Psalms 30:11 states "You turned my wailing into dancing; you removed my sackcloth and clothed me with joy", where God refers to dance as a form of joy.

The Liturgical Dance Ministry is used to assemble Godly dancers together to use the gift of dance to share the gospel of Jesus Christ through dance movement in worship. The ministry uses dance movements to encourage, comfort, and instruct various forms of faith. The dance ministry has the power to usher God's people into the spiritual realm of worship and freedom. The dancers must recognize that dance movements are used to minister and elevate the name of Jesus and not as a dance form of performance to promote self. In ministry a dancer is more than a dancer, in ministry a dancer is a worshipper that dances for God and has the desire to communicate a message from God. It is critical that in ministry, dancers understand and have the mindset and vocabulary of a worshipper.

Examples: (1) The dance ministry will minister to the song "God is My Everything". (2) She ministered today! (3) The church was in the spirit when the youth dancers ministered! (4) The Mime Ministry had ten mimers and they ministered! (5) "You better worship him!" But vocabulary is just the start of understanding the difference between dancing and ministering. There are specific characteristics that distinguish a dance ministry from a dance class: tithing, prayer, scripture, fasting, colors, garments, fellowship, and props.

Did you know that the art of dance began as a religious expression? Dance originally started in the church as a gospel expression, "history records that the first dance as religious rites performed in the early ancient cultures" (Curry, K., pp.11). Although there are various forms of dance used in worship; liturgical dance serves as the most accepted form of dance for praise and worship in the service.

Liturgical Dance is defined as a method of praise and worship through dance, that includes various forms of dance (ballet, jazz, hip-hop, African, stepping, and modern dance) movements. Liturgical dance has been widely accepted as a form of body movements used to demonstrate an expression of worship in a church setting.

> Liturgical dance is the decent and proper expression to God or from God (prophetic dance) through dance using music and choreography that attributes honor and glory to God. It is not enough to be a Christian and dance to any kind of music using any kind of choreography. Liturgical dance is used to be pure and perfect praise, specifically for the purpose of glorifying God. Its primary focus is to direct the congregation to God and to lead them into the worship. The focus is not the dancer, not the garment, not the choreography, the focus is GOD. (Curry, K., Dancing in the Spirit, pp.11)

CHAPTER IV

Styles Of Dance In Worship

Praise Dance is the primary form of liturgical dance used in the church service today. Praise dancing continues to grow in popularity using various dance movement, technique, and style. Praise dancing originated in the African American church and maintained an upbeat and fast form of liturgical and worship dancing. **Worship Dance** is a sacred form of liturgical dance, used to demonstrate the love of God. **Sacred Dance** is used to describe dance practiced by any religion. But liturgical, worship, praise, and gospel dancing are specific to the Christian church. **Gospel Dance** is a form of praise dance that originated from in the African American church. Gospel dance is dramatic and theatrical. **Warfare Dance** is a form of liturgical dance used to express and demonstrate a religious battle or religious war. The battle can demonstrate a battle with self, a battle to fight against sin, or a battle with the devil. A warfare dance uses movements that demonstrate fighting, breaking chains, and breaking strongholds. Black garments are typically used in warfare and mime dancing to symbolize battle, darkness, and the need for light, relief, and happiness.

 Mime Dance originated in ancient Greece, and the word mime is taken from a masked artist named Pantomimes. Miming is the art of conveying a message through exaggerated facial expressions, gestures, and body movements, without the use of words and verbal communication. Mime Dancers are also known for the painted white face and black garments. This form of garment is used to disguise and hide the natural face and draw all attention to body movements to present a dramatic and overly exaggerated presentation. Over the years, miming (mime dancing) has found its way into the church worship service demonstrating another form of praise, worship, and dance expression in ministry. Although the Bible does not specifically speak about mime as a form of dance, the Bible speaks to the concept of miming as imitations and impersonation. In **1 Corinthians 11:1**, the Bible says, "be imitators of me, just as I also am of Christ". **Romans 8:29** reads, "become conformed to the image of His Son".

CHAPTER V.
Governing Principles For The Dance Ministry

Governing principles are defined as a verbal, written, or implied agreements from established practice, that govern the purpose or operation of a program or organization and the rights and obligations of its membership. (Law Insider Dictionary). Where, there are governing principles that govern the successful operation of a dance ministry. These principles include tithing, praying, fasting, colors, garments, props, fellowship, fundraising, and life-long learning.

Spiritual Growth

The dance ministry leader is required to provide an opportunity and ensure spiritual growth for every member on the dance ministry and the leader is not exempt (including self). In **Hebrews 5:12**, the Bible reads "In fact, though by this time you ought to be teachers, you need someone to teach you the elementary truths of God's word all over again. You need milk, not solid food!" In 2 Peter 1:5, the Bible suggest "for this very reason, make every effort to add to your faith goodness; and to goodness, knowledge". The dance ministry leader must also recognize that spiritual growth extends beyond praying before and after dance practices; and extends beyond aligning the song to a bible scripture context.

Spiritual growth is simple, it is merely ensuring that each dancer grows spiritually and increases his or her faith. The Bible reads in **Ephesians 4:11-13**. (11) So, Christ himself gave the apostles, the prophets, the evangelists, the pastors and teachers, to equip his people for works of service, so that the body of Christ may be built up (12) To equip his people for works of service, so that the body of Christ may be built up. (13) Until we all reach unity in the faith and in the knowledge of the Son of God and become mature, attaining to the whole measure of the fullness of Christ. The ministry leader is obligated to ensure that all dancers understand and communicate with God through prayer, scripture reading, and bible study. Further in **Proverbs 1:4-5** the Bible reads, (4) For giving prudence to those who are simple, knowledge and discretion to the young. (5) Let the wise listen and add to their learning, and let the discerning get guidance (kjv).

Reflection

(1) What current practices do you use to ensure continued spiritual growth for self?

_____

_____

_____

_____

_____

_____

(2) What current practices do you implement to ensure that the dancers have continued spiritual growth?

_____

_____

_____

(3) Have you ever solicited guidance from a Pastor, Worship Leader, Minister, Dance Leader, or Mentor for spiritual growth recommendation? If YES, with who, when, and what was the recommendation and the outcome?

_____

_____

_____

_____

_____

_____

If No. Who can you collaborate with to ensure continued spiritual growth for self and the ministry dancers?

_____

_____

_____

(4) What can you do to enhance your program or what will you do differently to ensure that the ministry dancers have continued spiritual growth?

_____

_____

_____

_____

Principles of Spiritual Growth

1. Lead by example with intentional opportunities for spiritual growth.

2. Incorporate regular prayer time independently and with the ministry outside of dance rehearsals. In **Colossians 1:9** the Bible reads, "for this reason, since the day we heard about you, we have not stopped praying for you. We continually ask God to fill you with the knowledge of his will through all the wisdom and understanding that the Spirit gives."

3. Attend regular bible study with the dance ministry dancers. The Bible reads in **1 Timothy 4:13**, "until I come, devote yourself to the public reading of Scripture, to preaching and to teaching".

4. Facilitate regular discussions about bible scriptures, topics, and content. **1 Timothy 4:11**, "Command and teach these things".

5. Incorporate regular scripture reading and meditation for biblical understanding. **Proverbs 1:2**, "that gaining wisdom and instruction; for understanding words of insight."

6. Participate and facilitate Christian development courses, spiritual workshops, seminars, and other opportunities for spiritual growth. **Ephesians 4:21-22**, (21) when you heard about Christ and were taught in him in accordance with the truth that is in Jesus. (22) You were taught, with regard to your former way of life, to put off your old self, which is being corrupted by its deceitful desires.

7. Hold self and dancers to a higher standard of accountability for spiritual growth with associated consequences. **Luke 17:5**, The apostles said to the Lord, "Increase our faith!"

Create your Spiritual Growth Weekly Schedule. There is no right or wrong schedule. The schedule should challenge self and the ministry to grow, but also be realistic with measures of accountability. Do not set the ministry up for failure with unrealistic expectation, like the ministry will meet daily for bible study. That is unrealistic!

EXAMPLE: WEEKLY SPIRITUAL GROWTH SCHEDULE

	Day	Description/Activity
1	Monday	Independent Bible Reading, Studying, and Reflection.
2	Tuesday	OFF
3	Wednesday	Church Bible Study
4	Thursday	OFF
5	Friday	OFF
6	Saturday	Bible Study Review and Reflection with all Dancers.
7	Sunday	Church Service

Accountability may be that a dancer cannot minister if the dancer is not actively and regularly participating in bible study and attending church services. But accountability measures must apply to all dancers and leaders, no exceptions!

Create your Spiritual Growth Weekly Schedule for Self (Be specific).

	Day	Spiritual Growth Principle
1	Monday	
2	Tuesday	
3	Wednesday	
4	Thursday	
5	Friday	
6	Saturday	
7	Sunday	

Create a Spiritual Growth Weekly Schedule for the DANCERS.

	Day	Spiritual Growth Principle
1	Monday	
2	Tuesday	
3	Wednesday	
4	Thursday	
5	Friday	
6	Saturday	
7	Sunday	

Tithes and Tithing

Tithing is a tradition recognized by Christians and Jews that dates back to the Old Testament. Christians and Jews accepted that tithing is 10% of the gross income that should be given to the individuals church of membership. Tithes are used to support the expenses of the church. It is believed that the ten percent threshold came from the Hebrews meaning of the word tithe, that means a tenth. Christians and Jews practice tithing because it is biblical. And while it is important to give your time and your talents by doing things like ministering through dance, singing on the choir, serving the food bank, or knitting a blanket for a homeless person, the word tithe generally refers to giving of your personal financial resources at a rate of ten percent of your gross income.

Leviticus 27:30-32 (NIV)

30) A tithe of everything from the land, whether grain from the soil or fruit from the trees, belongs to the Lord; it is holy to the Lord.
31) Whoever would redeem any of their tithe must add a fifth of the value to it.
32) Every tithe of the herd and flock every tenth animal that passes under the shepherd's rod will be holy to the Lord.

Malachi 3:10 (NIV)

Bring the whole tithe into the storehouse, that there may be food in my house.

Deuteronomy 14:22-25 & 28 (NIV)

22) Be sure to set aside a tenth of all that your fields produce each year.
23) Eat the tithe of your grain, new wine and olive oil, and the firstborn of your herds and flocks in the presence of the Lord your God at the place he will choose as a dwelling for his Name, so that you may learn to revere the Lord your God always.
24) But if that place is too distant and you have been blessed by the Lord your God and cannot carry your tithe.
25) then exchange your tithe for silver and take the silver with you and go to the place the Lord your God will choose.
28) At the end of every three years, bring all the tithes of that year's produce and store it in your towns.

(1) Do you tithe? _____. Explain your answer.

_____

_____

_____

_____

_____

_____

(2) If you have questions or concerns about tithing, who can you talk to:

_____

_____

_____

_____

_____

_____

(3) Do you encourage the dancers to tithe? Explain your answer (when, how, and why).

_____

_____

_____

_____

_____

_____

Prayer and Fasting

Prayer and fasting work together. Prayer is the way humans communicate with God, through open dialogue. Fasting is a used to increase prayer time and time to communicate with God through prayer. People use fasting to deliberately reframe from eating or drinking in exchange for more prayer time and time to get closer to God. However, over the years fasting has grown to include reframing from almost anything: social media, television, candy, soft drinks, cigarettes, alcohol, relationships, and so much more. The Bible refers to prayer and fasting in both the old and new testaments. In the Old Testament, the Bible speaks about prayer and fasting in the Book of Psalms and Daniel. **Psalm 35:13** But I, when they were sick. I wore sackcloth; I afflicted myself with fasting; I prayed with head bowed on my chest. **Daniel 9:3** Then I turned my face to the Lord God, seeking him by prayer and pleas for mercy with fasting and sackcloth and ashes (ESV).

In the New Testament, the Bible speaks about prayer and fasting in the books of Luke and Acts. **Luke 2:37** And then as a widow until she was eighty-four. She did not depart from the temple, worshiping with fasting and prayer night and day. **Luke 5:33** And they said to him, "the disciples of John fast often and offer prayers, and so do the disciples of the Pharisees, but yours eat and drink. **Acts 13:2-3** While they were worshiping the Lord and fasting, the Holy Spirit said, "Set apart for me Barnabas and Saul for the work to which I have called them." Then after fasting and praying they laid their hands on them and sent them off. **Acts 14:23** And when they had appointed elders for them in every church, with prayer and fasting they committed them to the Lord in whom they had believed (ESV).

Prayer

According to Wikipedia, "Prayer is defined as an invocation or act that seeks to activate a rapport with an object of worship through deliberate communication." I describe prayer as man's tool to communicate with God, receive direction from God, and understand God's direction for your life. Through prayer people thank God for blessings. Through prayer, people seek forgiveness from God for their sins. Prayer is used to make request of God, intercede on behalf of others, seek happiness and completeness, and for anything else needed or desired from God. Traditionally, people got on their knees or kneeled at the alter to pray, but that is not a requirement people can pray anywhere, anytime, anyhow! God hears prayer!

The Bible speaks about prayer as a tool to communicate with God and a way to grow spiritually. "Rejoice always, pray without ceasing, give thanks in all circumstances; for this is the will of God in Christ Jesus for you"
1 Thessalonians 5:16-18.

☒ **Prayer for sin. 2 Chronicles 7:14** If my people, who are called by my name, will humble themselves and pray and seek my face and turn from their wicked ways, then I will hear from heaven, and I will forgive their sin and will heal their land. **1 John 5:16** If you see any brother or sister commit a sin that does not lead to death, you should pray and God will give them life. **James 5:16** Therefore confess your sins to each other and pray for each other so that you may be healed. The prayer of a righteous person is powerful and effective.

☒ **Prayer for Protection. John 17:15** My prayer is not that you take them out of the world but that you protect them from the evil one.

☒ **Prayer when in trouble. James 5:13** Is anyone among you in trouble? Let them pray. Is anyone happy? Let them sing songs of praise.

☒ **Answered prayers. Mark 11:24** Therefore I tell you, whatever you ask for in prayer, believe that you have received it, and it will be yours. **1 John 5:15** And if we know that he hears us—whatever we ask—we know that we have what we asked of him.

☒ **Prayer against temptation.** **Matthew 26:41** "Watch and pray so that you will not fall into temptation. The spirit is willing, but the flesh is weak."

☒ **Hear my prayers.** **Psalm 17:6 I** call on you, my God, for you will answer me; turn your ear to me and hear my prayer. **Psalm 102:17** He will respond to the prayer of the destitute; he will not despise their plea. **Proverbs 15:29** The LORD is far from the wicked, but he hears the prayer of the righteous. **Psalm 4:1** Answer me when I call to you, my righteous God. Give me relief from my distress; have mercy on me and hear my prayer. **Jeremiah 29:12** Then you will call on me and come and pray to me, and I will listen to you. **Job 22:27** You will pray to him, and he will hear you, and you will fulfill your vows. **Matthew 6:7** And when you pray, do not keep on babbling like pagans, for they think they will be heard because of their many words. **1 John 5:14** This is the confidence we have in approaching God: that if we ask anything according to his will, he hears us.

☒ **Devoted Prayer.** **Colossians 4:2** Devote yourselves to prayer, being watchful and thankful. **1 Thessalonians 5:17** pray continually. **1 Corinthians 7:5** Do not deprive one another, except perhaps by agreement for a limited time, that you may devote yourselves to prayer; but then come together again, so that Satan may not tempt you because of your lack of self-control (ESV).

☒ **Faithful prayer.** **Romans 12:12** Be joyful in hope, patient in affliction, faithful in prayer.

☒ **Prayer for the enemy.** **Matthew 5:44** But I tell you, love your enemies and pray for those who persecute you,

☒ **Pray for forgiveness.** **2 Chronicles 6:21** Hear the supplications of your servant and of your people Israel when they pray toward this place. Hear from heaven, your dwelling place; and when you hear, forgive.

✓ **Everyone must pray.** **1 Timothy 2:1-2** (1)I urge, then, first of all, that petitions, prayers, intercession and thanksgiving be made for all people. (2) for kings and all those in authority, that we may live peaceful and quiet lives in all godliness and holiness. **1 Timothy 2:8** Therefore I want the men everywhere to pray, lifting up holy hands without anger or disputing. **Luke 18:1** Then Jesus told his disciples a parable to show them that they should always pray and not give up.

☒ **Jesus prays.** Luke 6:12 One of those days Jesus went out to a mountainside to pray, and spent the night praying to God.

☒ **Prayer in weakness.** Romans 8:26 In the same way, the Spirit helps us in our weakness. We do not know what we ought to pray for, but the Spirit himself intercedes for us through wordless groans.

Reflection

1) Do you have a designated prayer room and time (please explain).

_____

_____

_____

_____

_____

_____

2) Do you believe that it is important to have scheduled regular daily prayer time?
Yes ( ) or No ( ) Please explain.

_____

_____

_____

_____

_____

(3) Have you shared with the dance ministry the importance of regularly scheduled prayer time?
Yes ( ) or No ( ) Please explain.

_____

_____

_____

_____

_____

(4) Do you require that the dance ministry come together for the sole purpose of prayer? ( ) Yes ( ) No
Explain your aswer.

_____

_____

_____

_____

_____

Fasting

The first mention of fasting was found in the Old Testament. Initially, fasting was used to demonstrate the self-restraint of consuming a specific food, in order to dedicate more time to communicate with God through prayer and studying God Word. Precisely, fasting was defined as a form of self-discipline that required an individual to deliberately reframe from eating for a designated timeframe, in efforts to communicate with God through prayer. It was suggested that fasting means to voluntarily decrease, reduce, or eliminate the consumption of food for a precise time, for a specific purpose. Fasting is done with purpose. I am fasting to communicate with God to seek forgiveness or to be more specific, I am fasting to seek forgiveness for my sins. Examples might include forgiveness for fornication, cursing, drinking, gossiping, stealing, lying, or any other sinful behavior.

In the Bible, the book of Daniel 10:2-3 reads,
(2) "In those days I, Daniel, was mourning for three weeks.
(3) I ate no delicacies, no meat or wine entered my mouth, nor did I anoint myself at all, for the full three weeks" (ESV).
Specifically, fasting was used to eliminate eating food and replace eating with quality prayer time with God. Fasting is used to free the mind and embrace God freely. Normally food is used when fasting. Specifically, people have been known to fast from meats, starch, sweats, caffeine, etc. Others have practiced fasting by eliminating a specific meal of the day, like fasting from breakfast or fasting from dinner. People have also implemented a food fast that designated times of day to reframe from eating, not eating from 5AM to 5PM or not eating from 6am to 12pm. But whatever the selected fast is, it should be something that is a challeng and requires discipline from the individual fasting. Fasting should not be easy. It should require dedication and commitment to be successful. Otherwise, the fast is a moot point and almost disrespectful to God.

⊠ Fasting and Sleep… Although food is the most common form of fasting, the Bible speaks to fasting and sleeping in II Corinthians 6:4-5.
(4) Rather, as servants of God we commend ourselves in every way: in great endurance; in troubles, hardships and distresses.
(5) In beatings, imprisonments, and riots; in hard work, sleepless nights and hunger. In II Corinthians 11:27, the Bible reads I have labored and toiled and have often gone without sleep; I have known hunger and thirst and have often gone without food; I have been cold and naked (NIV).

☒ **Fasting and Sex… I Corinthians 7:3-5**, the Bible speaks to fasting and re-framing from sex as a form of fasting. (3) The husband should fulfill his marital duty to his wife, and likewise the wife to her husband. (4) The wife does not have authority over her own body but yields it to her husband. In the same way, the husband does not have authority over his own body but yields it to his wife. (5) Do not deprive each other except perhaps by mutual consent and for a time, so that you may devote yourselves to prayer. Then come together again so that Satan will not tempt you because of your lack of self-control (NIV).

☒ **Motives for Fasting…**Fasting can be viewed as a symbol to demonstrate the need for God in someone's life. Fasting is also a way of asking God for help and sharing with God that you recognize that you cannot live without him. In **Isaiah 58:3-6** the Bible reads, (3) why have we fasted, they say, and you have not seen it? Why have we humbled ourselves, and you have not noticed? Yet on the day of your fasting, you do as you please and exploit all your workers. (4) Your fasting ends in quarreling and strife, and in striking each other with wicked fists. You cannot fast as you do today and expect your voice to be heard on high. (5) Is this the kind of fast I have chosen, only a day for people to humble themselves? Is it only for bowing one's head like a reed and for lying in sackcloth and ashes? Is that what you call a fast, a day acceptable to the Lord? (6) Is not this the kind of fasting I have chosen: to loose the chains of injustice and untie the cords of the yoke, to set the oppressed free and break every yoke (NIV)?

☒ **Fasted and God Answered…Ezra 8:23** So we fasted and petitioned our God about this, and he answered our prayer. **Joel 2:12** Yet even now, declares the Lord, "return to me with all your heart, with fasting, with weeping, and with mourning". **Acts 13:2** While they were worshiping the Lord and fasting, the Holy Spirit said, "Set apart for me Barnabas and Saul for the work to which I have called them" (ESV).

☒ **Fasting to Obtain Answers from God…Judges 20:26** Then all the Israelites, the whole army, went up to Bethel, and there they sat weeping before the Lord. They fasted that day until evening and presented burnt offerings and fellowship offerings to the Lord (NIV). **Ezra 8:21** Then I proclaimed a fast there, at the river Ahava, that we might humble ourselves before our God, to seek from him a safe journey for ourselves, our children, and all our goods (ESV).

☒ **The Fast of Choice…**As time progressed, fasting became more acceptable and allowed more flexibility in the choices of fast. In the Bible, **Isaiah 58:6-7** recorded that "Is not this the fast that I choose: to loose the bonds of wickedness, to undo the straps of the yoke, to let the oppressed go free, and to break every yoke?" (ESV)

☒ **Fasting for Repentance…1 Samuel 7:6** So they gathered at Mizpah and drew water and poured it out before the Lord and fasted on that day and said there, "We have sinned against the Lord." And Samuel judged the people of Israel at Mizpah. **1 Kings 21:27** And when Ahab heard those words, he tore his clothes and put sackcloth on his flesh and fasted and lay in sackcloth and went about dejectedly. **Joel 2:15** Blow the trumpet in Zion; consecrate a fast; call a solemn assembly (ESV).

☒ **Fasted and God Answered…Ezra 8:23** So we fasted and petitioned our God about this, and he answered our prayer. **Joel 2:12** Yet even now, declares the Lord, "return to me with all your heart, with fasting, with weeping, and with mourning". **Acts 13:2** While they were worshiping the Lord and fasting, the Holy Spirit said, "Set apart for me Barnabas and Saul for the work to which I have called them" (ESV).

☒ **The Biblical Forty-Day Fast…**Specifically, the Bible speaks to a forty day fast, in **Mark 1:13** And he was in the wilderness forty days, being tempted by Satan. And he was with the wild animals, and the angels were ministering to him. The Bible further mentions the forty day fast in **Deuteronomy 9:18** Then I lay prostrate before the Lord as before, forty days and forty nights. I neither ate bread nor drank water, because of all the sin that you had committed, in doing what was evil in the sight of the Lord to provoke him to anger. **Matthew 4:1-2** (1) Then Jesus was led up by the Spirit into the wilderness to be tempted by the devil. (2) And after fasting forty days and forty nights, he was hungry. **Exodus 34:28-29** (28) So he was there with the Lord forty days and forty nights. He neither ate bread nor drank water. And he wrote on the tablets the words of the covenant, the Ten Commandments. (29) When Moses came down from Mount Sinai, with the two tablets of the testimony in his hand as he came down from the mountain, Moses did not know that the skin of his face shone because he had been talking with God (kjv). **Luke 4:2** For forty days, being tempted by the devil. And he ate nothing during those days. And when they were ended, he was hungry (esv).

Reflection

(1) Do you practice fasting? ( ) Yes ( ) No. Please explain.

_____

_____

_____

_____

(2) Do you encourage the dancers to practice fasting?   Please explain.

_____

_____

_____

_____

_____

(3) Do you believe that fasting will help the dance ministry? Please explain.

_____

_____

_____

_____

(4) What bible scriptures support your thoughts about fasting?

_____

_____

_____

_____

_____

(5) Do you incorporate designated times in the year for the entire ministry to fast together?

Explain._____

_____

_____

_____

_____

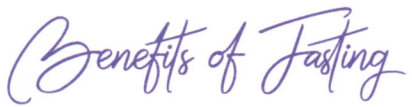
Benefits of Fasting

1. Fasting is most beneficial because it allows and enhances your time with God to pray.

2. Fasting is beneficial because it provides an opportunity to further understand God's word through prayer.

3. Fasting allows time to study the Word of God.

4. Fasting is beneficial to the body because it serves as a method of deliberate detoxing and elimination of toxins living in the body.

5. Fasting is beneficial because it is a public recognition that you are not a shame to share publicly that you need God.

6. Fasting is beneficial because it is a form of self-discipline.

7. Fasting is beneficial because it is a form of mental and spiritual focused development.

8. Fasting is beneficial because it provides a platform to hear from God clearly.

9. Fasting is beneficial because it provides an opportunity to fully focus on Jesus and not on self for growth and development.

10. Fasting is beneficial because it demonstrates respect for the mandates outlined in the bible.

11. Fasting is beneficial because it allows time to be closer to God.

12. Fasting is beneficial because it gives God your complete attention.

Reflection

(1) When was your last fast (date): _____

(2) Describe your last fast:

_____
_____
_____
_____
_____

(3) Was your last fast beneficial? Explain.

_____
_____
_____
_____
_____

(4) What if anything would you change about your last fast and why?

_____
_____
_____
_____
_____

(5) How will you introduce fasting to the dance ministry?

_____
_____
_____
_____
_____
_____

(6) What will the ministry fasting include and why?

_____

_____

_____

_____

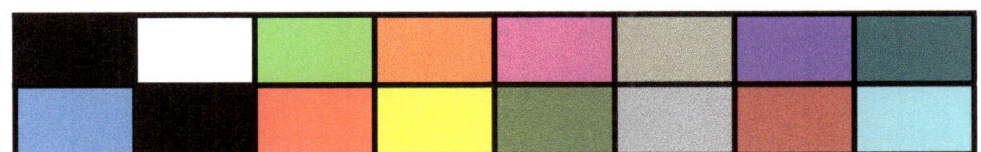

The Merriam Webster Dictionary defines color as:

> (1) a phenomenon of light or visual perception that enables one to differentiate otherwise identical objects. (2) the aspect of the appearance of objects and light sources that may be described in terms of hue, lightness, and saturation for objects and hue, brightness, and saturation for light sources.

Historically, colors have been used to describe various items, events, emotions, etc. In many cases colors have universal meanings that are accepted internationally. (1) White is used to symbolize a virgin, purity, snow, wedding bride, clear, clean, and Caucasians. (2) Red is globally used to symbolize blood, love, heart, fire, republican, and power. (3) Blue is globally recognized to describe a baby boy, sky, heaven, democrats, and water. (4) Pink is globally used to symbolize girls and breast cancer. (5) Green is used to symbolize money, plants, grass, vegetables, trees, and military. (6) Brown is used globally to symbolize dirt, dirty, earth, skin tones, and non-whites. (7) Black is used to symbolize African Americans, Mime, wartime, death, and mourning.

In many cases, Christians and other religious groups recognize colors and their meanings in the same manner as colors are used and defined in the secular world. Dance ministry leaders must understand the biblical meaning of colors and be selective when choosing a garment color that aligns with the lyrics and the meaning of the song to minister, because the song must be supported by scripture.

How do you currently select the garment colors for the ministry to use when ministering through dance?

_____

_____

_____

_____

_____

Meaning of Colors in Worship

Color	Meaning	Scriptural Basis
Black	Righteous Judgment, Sin, Death, Famine, Evil, Eternity, Death, Fear, Battle, Warfare, and Good Friday.	Lamentations 4:6-8
Blue	Heaven, Holy Spirit, Grace, Royalty, Water, Sky, Remembrance of God's Commands, River of Life, Peace, and Heaven.	Numbers 15:38, Esther 8:15
Brown	Earth, Humility, Dying, Decaying, and Atrophy.	Job 13:28, Habakkuk 3:16, 2 Corinthians 4:16
Gold	Glory of God, Royalty, Kingship, Wealth, Kingliness Refining Fire, the Godhead, Purification, Divinity, Majesty, Righteousness, Divine Light, and Mercy.	Esther 1:7
Gray	Ash, Repentance, Mortality of the Body, and the Immortality of the Spirit.	Isaiah 46:4-5, Psalm 71:18-19
Green	Healing, New Beginnings, Restoration, Life, Growth, Vigor, Hope, Freshness, and Prosperity.	Rev. 22:2, Hosea 14:8
Orange	Praise and Fire.	Exodus 27:1-4, Exodus 35:16, 1 Chron. 15:19
Pink	Right Relationship, Joy, and Compassion.	Ezekiel 11:19 Ezekiel 36:26
Purple	Royalty, Kingship, Majesty, Dignity, and King of Kings.	Judges 8:26
Red	Blood of Jesus, Spiritual Warfare, Salvation, Fire, Heart, and Love.	Rev. 12:11, Matthew 27:28, Nahum 2:3
Silver	Redemption, Strength, Faith, and Atonement.	Genesis 20:16, Matthew 27:2-9, Psalms 66:10
White	Purity, Innocence, Light, Beauty, Lamb of God, Appearance of God, Holiness, Conquest, Victory, Pure, Holy Spirit, Worship, Highest Praise, Completion, and Angels in Heaven.	Rev. 7:9, Psalm 51:7, Daniel 7:9, Rev 6:2
Yellow	God's Divine Glory, Presence of God, Sunshine, and Nature.	Ezekiel 1:4, 8:2

Color Quiz: Matching

Answer	Color			Meaning
1	White		A	Royalty, King of Kings
2	Blue		B	Warfare, Death, Fear
3	Purple		C	Fire, Blood, Heart, Love
4	Red		D	Heaven, Holy Spirit
5	Black		E	Purity, Pure, Grace

Song Choice and Color Examples:
1. Song: Will your heart and soul *"Say Yes"* (by Michelle Williams) garment color choice might include RED to represent the heart.
2. Song: *"Break Every Chain"* (by Tarsha Cobb Leonard) garment color might include BLACK to represent the breaking of chains and strongholds.
3. Song: *"Shift in the Atmosphere"* (by Jason Nelson) garment color might include BLUE or PURPLE to represent the atmosphere.
4. Song: *"The Blood Still Works"* (by Malcolm Williams) garment color might include RED to represent the blood of Jesus.
5. Song: *"King of Kings"* (by Hillsong Worship) garment color might include PURPLE or GOLD to represent royalty of kings.
6. Song: *"Grateful"* (by Hezekiah Walker) garment color might include WHITE to represent the highest level of worship.
7. Song: *"Total Praise"* (Richard Smallwood) garment color might include WHITE to represent praise to God.
8. Song: *"Church of Fire"* (by Hillsong Worship) garment color might include combinations of RED, ORANGE and YELLOW to represent the fire.
9. Song: *"Melodies from Heaven"* (by Kirk Franklin) garment color might include BLUE to represent heaven.
10. Song: *"Wade in the Water"* (by Ramsey Lewis) garment color might include BLUE to represent the water.

Matching Quiz Answer Key: (1) E, (2) D, (3) A, (4) C, (5) B

Reflection

(1) How will you educate and share the definition of colors with the dancers?

_____

_____

_____

_____

_____

(2) Now, that you have a better understanding of the use of colors in worship, what process will you use to select garment colors for the dance worship experience?

STEPS

1._____

2._____

3._____

4._____

5._____

6._____

7._____

8._____

9._____

10._____

PRACTICE 1: Garment Selection Process. Based on the key lyrics of a song of your choice, identify a supporting scripture and then select a garment color to use in ministry through dance.

Step 1: Song & Artist _____

Step 2: Listen and meditate on the song.

Step 3: Identify the key lyrics of the song chosen to minister _____

_____

_____

Step 4: Identify a supporting Bible scripture _____

_____

_____

_____

_____

Step 5: : What does the aligned scripture mean _____

_____

_____

Step 6: : Identify an appropriate garment color to describe the song and explain

_____

_____

PRACTICE 2

(1) Select a Gospel Song _____

(2) What are the key lyrics in the song?

_____

_____

_____

_____

_____

(3) What does the song mean? What message is the artist trying to convey?

_____

_____

_____

(4) Identify scriptures to support the key lyrics in the song:

_____

_____

_____

(5) How does the selected scripture align with the song?

_____

_____

_____

(6) What colors support the song, scripture, and key lyrics? How?

_____

_____

_____

PRACTICE 3 Select the color that best support the song and why.
Example: Song: "Millionaire" by Tauren Wells and Kirk Franklin.
Color: green to represent money and millionaire.

1. Song: Deliver Me (Donald Lawrence). Color: _____

Why: _____

_____

2. Song: Shackles (Mary Mary). Color: _____

Why: _____

_____

3. Song: Praise is What I Do (William Murphy). Color: _____

Why: _____

_____

4. Song: I Smile (Kirk Franklin). Color: _____

Why: _____

_____

5. Song: My God (Jordan Armstrong). Color: _____

Why: _____

_____

What Dancers should know about Garments?

The garment in simple terms refer to the dancer's clothing worn to minister through dance. Clothing is described as garments, clothes, apparel, and attire all representing items worn to cover the body. Typically, clothing is made of various fabrics and textiles and displayed in various colors. Wearing clothing is a social norm, used for various purposes. In the secular realm, clothing is used to cover the body, keep the body warm, and protect the skin from elements of the world: insects, plants, rain, smoke, fire, allergies, cold, hot, snow, toxins, and the sun.

Clothing creates a barrier between the human skin and the environment. In many parts of the world clothing is mandatory and lack of clothing can be embarrassing and, in some cases, considered indecent exposure. The same premise applies to clothing worn to dance, where the terms clothing, costumes, and garments work interchangeably depending on the type of dance. Precisely, liturgical and praise dancers refer to the dance attire as dance garments.

Dance styles naturally have their own recommended attire or garments, carefully chosen to compliment the style of dance and to allow for easy movement based the style of dance. In the article, Liturgical *Dance as a Form of Worship*, Treva Bedinghaus wrote:

> Rather than tights and leotards designed to help the audience focus on the dancers' line and form. Praise dancers wear loose-fitting, modest attire, aimed at keeping the audience's attention on the spiritual message they are trying to convey through their movements, rather than the bodies being used to convey it".

A typical praise dance garment might include an undergarment such as a leotard, tights, leggings, worn beneath a loose-fitting overlay, top, or cape with palazzo pants, circle skirt or both (Pants and skirt). It is recommended that both male and female dancers wear loose or palazzo pants. But female dancers are also encouraged to compliment the palazzo pants with a circle skirt, to provide more coverage and exaggeration of dance movement.

The dance garment is the introduction to the dance worship experience. The garment is the initial exposure to the dance worship experience. The garment sets the tone as to how the dancer will be accepted or lack of acceptance. Before the dancer implements one dance move the garment has already communicated something to the audience. It is the dancer's responsibility to ensure that the garment compliments and aligns with the vision of the dance. The last thing a dancer wants to do, is to wear a garment that is a distraction to the dance worship experience. Believe it or not, the garment choice is more important than the choreography. The wrong garment selection can hinder the dancer's ability to worship through dance.

Therefore, dancers must realize that the garment must be anointed and covered with prayer. Garments should never be worn in the streets as part of street attire. Garments should be clean and protected and only revealed when used for ministry and worship. Garments should be prayerfully selected, tasteful in style, color, and appropriately fitted for all dancers. Dancers must realize that store bought garments are not always made for all dancers. A dancer must be honest with self and recognize the pros and cons of his/her figure and tailor garments accordingly.

Example: If a dancer is top heavy (large breasted) the dancer may want to consider a mock neck or turtleneck leotard. Where a small breasted female can wear a regular round neck leotard. In this example if the ministry is requiring that all dancers have identical garments then the ministry should lean towards accommodating the dancer with the larger breast. But this process must be implemented when selecting all garments.

But liturgical garments can be costly and building a dance ministry wardrobe can be expensive and may for many be difficult to purchase. Unfortunately, the garment required pieces are not negotiable, one negotiated garment piece could hinder the ministry's ability to worship through dance, ultimately hindering the ability to SHEPHERD IN THE HOLY SPIRIT & SAVE A SOUL!

So how does a dance ministry leader build a dance ministry wardrobe? Typically, the white garment is the foundation for starting a liturgical dancer's garment wardrobe. The ministry can acquire various overlays (styles and colors) to compliment the white garment foundation to build a liturgical dancer's garment wardrobe.

NOTE: EVERY LITURIGICAL DANCER should be REQUIRED to have a COMPLETE WHITE GARMENT foundation:

1. **White** Long Sleeve Leotard
2. **White** Tights or Leggings
3. **White** Palazzo Pants
4. **White** Liturgical Skirt or Liturgical Dress (Women Only)
5. **White** Liturgical Praise Overlay

As the ministry continues to grow its financial resources, ministry, and worship experiences; the ministry may want to also consider acquiring a COMPLETE BLACK GARMENT foundation that can be used to better set the atmosphere for warfare ministry and worship. The black garment foundation can also be used to compliment various overlays or identical overlays as used with the white garment foundation.

1. **Black** Long Sleeve Leotard
2. **Black** Tights or Leggings
3. **Black** Palazzo Pants
4. **Black** Liturgical Skirt or Liturgical Dress (Women Only)
5. **Black** Liturgical Praise Overlay

It is recommended that new dance ministries start with a complete undisturbed white garment. For women that includes white leotard, white tights or leggings, white skirt or white dress, white palazzo pants, and a white overlay. For men that includes white undershirt, white sport tights or leggings, white palazzo pants, and white overlay. For the purpose of building a garment wardrobe the white garment can be worn for all dancers. Recognizing that specific colors outside of white may better compliment the song choice. For example, adding red to the white garment, when dancing to a song about your heart or the blood of Jesus. However, if the ministry has limited garments, all white is always acceptable.

As a garment expert for liturgical dance ministries, it is my recommendation that new dance ministries start with a complete undisturbed white garment, to serve as the garment wardrobe foundation for the ministry. The white garment can typically be worn for most dances, although specific colors outside of white may better compliment the dance. However, the white garment will not distract from the ministry worship experience. The white garment is the start and can be used to build the garment wardrobe.

Garment Do's and Don'ts

1. Dancers should always be fully covered and NEVER reveal anything sexual.
2. Makeup should be tasteful, lightly applied, and of natural colors and tones.
3. Fingernail and Toenail polishes should be neutral colors and neatly applied.
4. Praise Dancers should always wear a leotard and leggings or tights under the garment.
5. Palazzo or dance pants are highly recommended for Praise Dancers (male and female).
6. Garments should NEVER be tight or revealing in any form.
7. Dancers should NEVER allow breast nipples to show (male/female).
8. Dancers with protruding nipples must be creative to ensure that nipples are NEVER seen, use band aids, padded bras, double bras, ace bandages, etc.
9. Large breasted women must ensure that the breast are secured with limited or no movement ability while ministering through dance.
10. Large breasted women may require expensive or double bras for security.
11. A female's silhouette should NEVER be revealed through a praise dance garment, dancers may need to layer garments or purchase larger garments.
12. Male dancers should wear jock straps or sports briefs to secure and stabilize the penis and testicles.
13. Hair styles should be tasteful (male/female).
14. Female dancer's hair should be secured, pinned up, in a bun, and off of the face.
15. Male dancer's hair should be groomed, cut, trimmed, and neatly secured off of the face.
16. Hair color should be a neutral color for male and female dancers.
17. Tattoos should NEVER be visible while ministering through dance.
18. Full figured dancers should consider body shapers or girdles to eliminate and avoid unwanted body movements, shaking, and giggling.
19. Garment fit should be tasteful to avoid tight, form-fitting, revealing, too loose, sloppy, or a big fit.
20. Praise Dancers should wear a circle skirt or dress and palazzo pants when ministering, regardless of overlay style.
21. All dancers (male and female) should wear appropriate undergarments.
22. Females must use necessary extra precautions when menstruating.
23. A dancer's feet should be clean, moisturized, or covered with dance shoes.
24. Underwear garments to avoid (male/female): thongs, booty shorts, bikinis, lace, satin, exotic, G-strings, garters, chiffon, open-crochet, butt-lift, bright colors, florals, ultra-thin, etc.

25. Females should wear panties that cover the entire buttocks and vagina area.

26. Males should wear underwear that cover the entire buttocks, penis, and testicles.

27. Males should always wear a full under shirt or tee shirt, to protect against unwanted visual underarm and body perspiration.

Worship Dance Garments

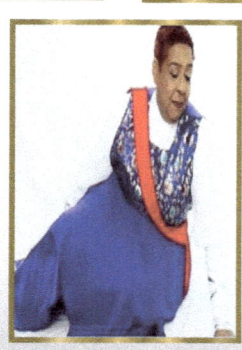

Garment Crossword Puzzle

A	F	F	A	B	R	I	C	S	V	N	E	B	B	G	N	N	P	R	A	I	S	E
S	F	A	R	Y	A	Z	J	G	Y	O	K	L	S	Z	O	A	A	G	J	I	P	L
C	G	A	R	M	E	N	T	A	U	Y	D	A	H	L	K	E	I	L	H	R	A	E
R	S	Q	B	J	O	K	A	R	N	F	O	C	A	K	B	I	N	B	E	A	L	O
T	A	I	S	R	U	S	W	M	D	R	C	K	P	U	L	O	T	K	U	I	A	T
A	P	C	K	C	I	S	H	O	E	A	Y	B	U	Y	A	U	F	C	Y	S	Z	R
I	O	T	I	M	N	E	T	T	R	I	B	R	K	O	C	S	Z	C	T	E	Z	R
L	G	A	R	N	Y	A	W	U	G	G	A	I	E	E	G	N	O	O	A	D	O	D
O	A	I	T	N	Z	E	L	H	A	W	M	C	R	A	V	E	Z	N	Y	E	D	B
R	R	B	U	C	D	A	I	W	R	H	R	S	L	S	C	Y	D	M	C	T	L	Y
R	M	V	T	U	F	R	F	A	M	I	B	F	K	A	A	C	R	S	C	T	O	A
W	O	R	S	H	I	P	I	S	E	A	B	A	C	L	B	U	L	R	A	H	N	L
O	Z	A	W	Z	R	R	T	H	N	M	G	W	R	G	C	E	O	A	L	W	G	Y
R	N	A	O	U	E	A	N	F	T	O	B	E	Z	S	A	S	A	I	B	L	S	A
H	C	B	R	M	C	L	Z	N	Y	G	V	O	A	V	P	R	A	S	E	P	L	R
I	S	E	H	C	O	B	M	N	O	O	D	B	E	Z	Z	F	L	G	G	C	E	E
P	H	W	P	B	D	D	A	N	C	C	E	R	P	R	A	E	S	P	G	E	E	V
S	A	H	W	A	O	B	L	L	I	T	U	R	G	I	C	A	L	N	W	U	V	O
A	P	I	H	Z	O	C	E	A	P	Y	G	R	B	N	U	Q	O	B	B	B	E	R
C	E	T	I	G	H	T	S	E	E	V	E	G	O	R	B	L	R	A	N	C	H	L
B	Q	E	P	R	A	I	E	S	T	P	Z	J	L	E	O	T	A	R	D	A	N	D
B	O	D	Y	S	H	A	P	E	R	F	O	H	S	H	O	T	U	U	W	R	U	P
O	P	L	A	Z	O	O	N	A	T	U	R	A	L	N	A	C	B	B	S	F	B	W

Props in Ministry

Words

Black	Garment	Overlay	Skirt
Body Shaper	Liturgical	Palazzo	Tailor
Bun	Leotard	Paint	Undergarment
Fabrics	Long Sleeve	Praise	White
Fire	Natural	Shoe	Worship

Props in Ministry used to enhance the worship experience!

The section is designed to offer a biblical foundation for the use of props in the praise dance worship experience. In ministry props are physical items included in the dance to set the atmosphere and to usher in the Holy Spirit. Dances may incorporate flags, streamers, banners, billows, wings, handkerchief, timbrels, crowns, the Bible, and many other items in efforts to better communicate the message from God. These props are used in praise and worship to set the atmosphere and usher in the holy spirit. Flags are the most commonly used props in praise and worship dances.

saiah 13:2, the Bible reads "Lift ye up a banner upon the high mountain, exalt the voice unto them, shake the hand, that they may go into the gates of the nobles. Flags are also used to build the kingdom of God and break down things that are not of God". Further in Isaiah 62:10, the Bible suggest "go through, go through the gates; prepare ye the way of the people; cast up, cast up the highway; gather out the stones; lift up a standard for the people. Flags and Banners are further used to demonstrate victory granted by God". Zechariah 9:16 the Bible states that "the Lord their God shall save them in that day as the flock of his people: for they shall be as the stones of a crown, lifted up as an ensign upon his land. (KJV).

(1) What are your thoughts about dance props for dance ministry :

_____

_____

_____

(2) How do you train dancers to use props?

_____

_____

_____

(3) List examples of when props are appropriate and why?

    a. _____

    b. _____

    c. _____

    d. _____

    e. _____

    f. _____

"Praise Dancers fly with or without wings!"

~drs

Mentorship

How do you define mentorship?

_____

_____

_____

_____

_____

A mentor serves in an identical capacity of a counselor. Mentors and Counselors are described as informed trustworthy individuals. Mentors are used in multiple roles and under various circumstances. Mentors are most common in school settings. But the mentor role can be extended and has deemed to be relevant and successful in many areas. The mentor is often referred to as the leader or the teacher, in the collaborative relationship. The student is referred to as the mentee, and together they form a relationship that is referred to as mentorship.

"Mentorship is a relationship in which a more experienced or more knowledgeable person helps to guide a less experienced or less knowledgeable person. The mentor may be older or younger than the person being mentored, but they must have a certain area of expertise" (Wikipedia). Mentoring is important, not only because of the knowledge and skills shared by the mentor with the mentee but also because mentoring provides professional socialization and personal support to facilitate the success of the mentee. "Quality mentoring greatly enhances students' chances for success" (Bellows and Perry, 2005).

Often times the mentor uses his or her personal development experiences to guide the mentor/mentee relationship. The mentor may share with a mentee information about his or her past, career path, family, education, as well as provide guidance, motivation, emotional support, and serve as a role model for the mentee. A mentor will guide the mentee through career selections, establishing goals, and providing a community network, developing pertinent contacts, and identifying resources needed for success. Most importantly, a mentor plays a critical role in the development of the mentee's self-esteem.

Reflection

(1) How do you think a mentorship relationship can enhance the dance ministry? Explain.

_____

_____

_____

(2) Why do you think mentors are important to the dancers? Explain.

_____

_____

_____

(3) Do you currently mentor the dancers? Explain.

_____

_____

_____

(4) How do you currently mentor each dancer in the dance ministry, be specific? There are no right or wrong answers, this will help you as the dance ministry leader understand the ministry strengths and weakness individually and collectively in efforts to improve the dance ministry.

Dancer 1 _____

_____

_____

Dancer 2 _____

_____

_____

Dancer 3 _____

_____

_____

Dancer 4_____

_____

_____

Dancer 5_____

_____

_____

Dancer 6_____

_____

_____

Dancer 7_____

_____

_____

Dancer 8_____

_____

_____

What we know, is that the mentor, mentee mentorship is critical to the success of the mentee in a general sense. What we also know is that the mentor mentee mentorship is a relationship between what is known as the teacher and the student or the leader and the follower. So, when we put the mentor-mentee mentorship in the context of a dance ministry, the meanings are identical. The dance ministry leader serves as the mentor and dancer is the mentee and it is the responsibility of the mentor, to mentor and guide the mentee. The dance ministry leader (mentor) can be instrumental in both the self-esteem and dance technique development of a dancer (mentee). The dance ministry leader (mentor) is accountable for ensuring that the mentee or dancer excels to the dancers greatest desired potential on the dance ministry.

(5) What steps will you implement with new dancers to the ministry, to start the dancer and leader mentor relationship.

_____

_____

_____

The dance ministry leader (mentor) should have five traits:

(1) Empower
(2) Encourage
(3) Life Skills
(4) Core Values
(5) Interpersonal Skills

1. **EMPOWER.** The dance ministry leader (mentor) empowers the dancer (mentee) to make positive choices. The mentor empowers the mentee to consider possible positive and negative outcomes and consequences of his or her choices in advance.

How can you empower the dance ministry dancers?

_____

_____

_____

_____

2. **ENCOURAGE.** A dance ministry leader (mentor) encourages the dancer (mentee) to take ownership of his or her education and development. The mentor provides multiple opportunities and options for the mentee to develop. The mentor will suggest challenges that push the mentee to higher levels mentally, emotionally, physically, and professionally. The ultimate goal of a mentor is to prepare the mentee and serve as a coach in all situations: sports, school, church, work, home, and life itself.

How can you encourage the dancers to take ownership of his or her continued development?

_____

_____

_____

_____

3. LIFE SKILLS. A dance ministry leader (mentor) helps the dancer (mentee) to develop life skills. The mentor guides the mentee in setting goals, objectives, addressing challenges, and developing techniques to manage emotions.

As a mentor, how can you assist dancers with developing goals and objectives (regardless of the age of the dancer)?

_____

_____

_____

_____

4. CORE VALUES. " Core values are traits or qualities that are not just worthwhile, they represent an individual's or an organization's highest priorities, deeply held beliefs, and core, fundamental driving forces. They are the heart of what your organization and its employees stand for in the world." (https://www.thebalancecareers.com)

A dance leader mentor helps the dancer mentee develop core values to apply to the dance experience. A mentor will help the mentee establish core values that will govern the dancer's future. "Mentors should guide youth to understand and develop key values. Our coaches help participants learn, The First Nine Core Values: honesty, integrity, sportsmanship, respect, confidence, responsibility, perseverance, courtesy, and judgment" (The Power of Mentorship).

How will you educate and promote core values in the dancers?

_____

_____

_____

_____

5. INTERPERSONAL SKILLS. A dance ministry leader mentor strengthens the dancer's mentee interpersonal skills. The mentor is responsible for training and nurturing the mentee to appreciate diversity, equity, self-respect, self-love, respect, and love for others. The mentor is also charged with assisting the mentee with his/her development of interpersonal skills, skills needed to enhance interactions with others.

How can the dance ministry leader assist the dancers with understanding and strengthening interpersonal skills?

_____

_____

_____

_____

Is it the dance ministry leader's responsibility to mentor the dancers to ensure that each dancer reaches his or her highest potential? Yes _____   No _____

Why? _____

_____

_____

_____

_____

Mentorship is so critical because an educated and confident dancer will dance with confidence and offer a more spiritual dance experience for self and others. As the dance leader you are responsible for the full development of each dancer. Often times dancers look to the dance ministry leader with an expectation, that as the leader, the leader will make the dancer a better dancer. But as the dance ministry leader, you must understand that you are required to educate the dancers about the purpose of the dance ministry and the role of each dancer in the ministry.   This is accomplished through the mentorship relationship between the leader and the dancer.

What will you do differently as the mentor (leader) to ensure the success of your mentees (dancers)? List each dancer separately.

_____

_____

_____

_____

_____

_____

Fellowship

In ministry, fellowship is defined as a group of like religious individuals, casually coming together for the purpose of entertainment. Fellowships are normally implemented outside of the normal business of the ministry. Fellowships are used to congregate in an informal comfortable setting to become better acquainted with one another. The fellowship setting also provides an opportunity to become informed about each dancer on the ministry outside of the dance experience. Fellowship is discussed throughout the bible in the Old and New Testament.

The Bible specifically describes fellowship in 1 John 1:3. That which we have seen and heard we proclaim also to you, so that you too may have fellowship with us; and indeed our fellowship is with the Father and with his Son Jesus Christ. 1 John 1:7. But if we walk in the light, as he is in the light, we have fellowship with one another, and the blood of Jesus his Son cleanses us from all sin. Acts 2:42. And they devoted themselves to the apostles' teaching and the fellowship, to the breaking of bread and the prayers. 1 John 1:7. But if we walk in the light, as he is in the light, we have fellowship with one another, and the blood of Jesus his Son cleanses us from all sin. Acts 2:42. And they devoted themselves to the apostles' teaching and the fellowship, to the breaking of bread and the prayers. 1 Corinthians 1:9. God is faithful, by whom you were called into the fellowship of his Son, Jesus Christ our Lord (ESV).

1 John 1:3. That which we have seen and heard we proclaim also to you, so that you too may have fellowship with us; and indeed our fellowship is with the Father and with his Son Jesus Christ. 1 John 1:6-7. If we say we have fellowship with him while we walk in darkness, we lie and do not practice the truth. But if we walk in the light, as he is in the light, we have fellowship with one another, and the blood of Jesus his Son cleanses us from all sin. 2 Corinthians 13:14. The grace of the Lord Jesus Christ and the love of God and the fellowship of the Holy Spirit be with you all. 1 John 1:7. But if we walk in the light, as he is in the light, we have fellowship with one another, and the blood of Jesus his Son cleanses us from all sin. 1 John 1:3. That which we have seen and heard we proclaim also to you, so that you too may have fellowship with us; and indeed our fellowship is with the Father and with his Son Jesus Christ (ESV).

The Bible speaks to the **purpose of a fellowship** in 1 Thessalonians 5:11 therefore encourage one another and build one another up, just as you are doing. Hebrews 10:25. Not neglecting to meet together, as is the habit of some, but encouraging one another, and all the more as you see the Day drawing near. **Psalm 133:1.** A Song of Ascents. Of David. Behold, how good and pleasant it is when brothers dwell in unity. **1 Peter 3:8.** Finally, all of you, have unity of mind, sympathy, brotherly love, a tender heart, and a humble mind. **Acts 2:44.** And all who believed were together and had all things in common. **Acts 2:46.** And day by day, attending the temple together and breaking bread in their homes, they received their food with glad and generous hearts, praising God and having favor with all the people (ESV).

Romans 1:12. That is, that we may be mutually encouraged by each other's faith, both yours and mine. **Hebrews 10:24-25.** And let us consider how to stir up one another to love and good works, not neglecting to meet together, as is the habit of some, but encouraging one another, and all the more as you see the Day drawing near. **Colossians 3:16.** Let the word of Christ dwell in you richly, teaching and admonishing one another in all wisdom, singing psalms and hymns and spiritual songs, with thankfulness in your hearts to God. **Acts 2:44.** And all who believed were together and had all things in common. **Acts 1:14.** All these with one accord were devoting themselves to prayer, together with the women and Mary the mother of Jesus, and his brothers. **2 Corinthians 6:14.** Do not be unequally yoked with unbelievers. For what partnership has righteousness with lawlessness? Or what fellowship has light with darkness (ESV)?

Reflection

(1) How do you define fellowship?

_____

_____

_____

(2) Does the ministry have "regular" fellowships? Yes ( ) or No ( ) Explain your answer.

_____

_____

_____

(3) The Bible commands that we fellowship. Do you believe fellowships are important for the dance ministry? Explain.

_____

_____

_____

_____

(4) When was the dance ministries last fellowship? _____

(5) Describe the last dance ministry fellowship? What were the outcomes of the fellowship. Explain.

_____

_____

_____

_____

(6) What will you do differently (if anything), as it relates to fellowships with the dance ministry:

_____

_____

_____

Fundraising

Fundraising is defined as the process of seeking financial support for a charity, cause, or other enterprise. In ministry fundraising is defined as soliciting and acquiring funding from others outside of the ministry in efforts to off set cost for the ministry. (dictionary.cambridge.org)

One might say why is it the responsibility of the Dance Ministry Leader and Dancers to raise money? It's simple, there is nothing like your own money and dance ministers need money! The goal of fundraising in the church is meant to raise money to address a need within the church that is normally not covered by tithes and offerings. Fundraising is giving in addition to tithing. In **Corinthians 9:7**, the Bible reads "each one must give as he has decided in his heart, not reluctantly or under compulsion, for God loves a cheerful giver." Additionally, churches are nonprofit organizations, primarily funded by its membership that includes the dance ministry dancers. Ultimately meaning that the dancers already have a 10% tithe monetary responsibility to the church outside of the dance ministry. Where, as you can imagine, the dance ministry is a costly ministry and the most devasting experience as a dance ministry leader is to learn that someone cannot minister through dance because that person cannot afford to participate and purchase the necessary dance garments.

This is why fundraising imperative. A dance ministry should always maintain a basic inventory of garments to ensure that anyone that has the desire to minister through dance can. It is also, good to have funds available for the dancers to travel to other churches and events that may improve the ministry and offer exposure in the community. Further, a dance ministry may be required to purchase props, flags, banners, wings, streamers, lighting, music, equipment, backdrops, bibles, etc. to enhance the ministry experience.

Reflection

(1) Does the dance ministry raise money through fundraising? YES ( ) or No ( )
If yes, what are some of the fundraising initiatives implemented by the dance ministry?

_____

_____

_____

(2) What was the most profitable dance ministry fundraiser project:

_____

_____

_____

(3) What was the profit? _____

(4) How did you motivate the dancers to participate in the fundraiser?

_____

_____

_____

(5) Why was this fundraiser so successfully? Who was involved?

_____

_____

_____

(6) How did you use the money raised?

_____

_____

_____

(7) Do you have a fundraising plan for the dance ministry? Yes ( ) or No ( )

(8) What fundraising ideas are you planning to implement in the next 3 years?

_____

_____

_____

(9) What is the projected monetary fundraising goal?

_____

(10) How do you plan to motivate the dancers to participate in future fundraising projects?

_____

_____

_____

_____

_____

(11) What are the plans for any money raised through fundraising?

_____

_____

_____

_____

_____

Life-Long Learner

A lifelong learner is an individual dedicated to continued unlimited learning. A lifelong learner is an individual that is self-motivated to grow through personal and professional development. Lifelong learning in most cases is based on an individuals desire to learn (professional development) outside of post-secondary education at the college degree level (associate, bachelor, master, or doctorate degrees). Lifelong learning can be education for personal interest or professional ambitious in efforts to support or fulfill an independent goal.

Lifelong Learning Options for Dancers:

- Dance Technique Classes or Program
- Fitness Classes or Program
- Yoga Classes or Program
- Ballet and Modern Dance Classes or Program
- African Dance Classes or Program
- Bible Study or Biblical Training
- Leadership Training
- Choreography
- Mentorship and Coaching
- Flagging and Streaming
- Balancing and Gymnastics
- Fundraising

Are you a lifelong learner? If yes, what makes you a lifelong learner?

_____

_____

_____

_____

How will lifelong learning support the dance ministry?

_____

_____

_____

_____

What lifelong learning activities have you participated in the last year?

1. _____

2. _____

3. _____

4. _____

5. _____

How do you share acquired knowledge with the dance ministry members?

_____

_____

_____

_____

Life-Long Learner

"Twelve Powerful Habits of a Lifelong Learner"

by Oskar Nowik

YES	NO	The core habits to self-improvement.
		1) **They Read on a Daily Basis.** Lifelong learners are well read and stay current.
		2) **They Attend Various Courses.** Lifelong learners are constantly seeking opportunities to participate and develop through formal educational or professional development opportunities.
		3) **They Actively Seek Opportunities to Grow.** Lifelong learners are constantly exploring opportunities to grow or explore higher level opportunities.
		4) **They Take Care of Their Bodies.** Lifelong learners recognize the importance of good health and wellness. "Physical fitness is not only one of the most important keys to a healthy body, it is the basis of dynamic and creative intellectual activity." — John F. Kennedy. Lifelong learners understand that a healthy body is key to the development of the mind that translates into success.
		5) **They Have Diverse Passions.** A lifelong learner understands the importance of diversity, maintaining a diverse portfolio, practicing different skills, and maintaining advantage over others.
		6) **They Love Making Progress.** Lifelong learners love to experience the constant growth and improvement. The breakthrough moments help them to notice the impressive change that took place because of the learning process. Any milestone serves as a driving force for further headway.
		7) **They Challenge Themselves with Specific Goals.** Lifelong learners function using clearly defined goals. Lifelong learners challenge themselves to reach their highest potential.
		8) **They Embrace Change.** As a lifelong learner, you know a change can lead to extraordinary results so you welcome it and stay open minded about making a shift.
		9) **They Believe It's Never Too Late to Start Something.** Some people tend to think after a certain age, they are no longer allowed to start something and become successful. The truth is, it's just a lame excuse not to leave your comfort zone.
		10) **Their Attitude to Getting Better Is Contagious.** As a life long learner, you are extremely passionate about the constant growth and people around you can sense that positive attitude. As a result, they start acting similarly.
		11) **They Leave Their Comfort Zone.** Every time you get out of your comfort zone, regardless whether you win or fail, you learn something new. That's the part you love the most!
		12) **They Never Settle Down. Lifelong learners never settle.** Without a doubt, you appreciate what you already know, but that's never a reason to stop. You just know once you stop learning, you lose the amazing privilege humans have, namely an ability to a never-ending intellectual development.

How do you measure? Do you practice the twelve powerful habits of a lifelong learner?   Yes _____   No_____

What are your strong areas as outlined in the "Twelve Powerful Habits of a Lifelong Learner:

_____

_____

_____

_____

_____

What habits do you need to improve?

_____

_____

_____

_____

_____

How will you improve in those areas?

_____

_____

_____

_____

_____

"The colors are another expression of the dance!"

~ drs

Dance Ministry Practice

What does the Bible say about praise dancing?

Psalms 149:3-4 Let them praise His name with the dance. Let them sing praises to Him with the timbrel and harp. For the Lord takes pleasure in His people. He will beautify the humble with Salvation.

What does the Bible say about practice?

Philippians 4:9 What you have learned and received and heard and seen in me—practice these things, and the God of peace will be with you.

Matthew 6:1 Beware of practicing your righteousness before other people in order to be seen by them, for then you will have no reward from your Father who is in heaven.

1 Timothy 4:15 Practice these things, immerse yourself in them, so that all may see your progress.

What is a dance practice?

A dance practice is a purposeful meeting, for the primary purpose of choreography and repetitious training of dance movements in preparation for ministry through dance. A dance practice consists of welcome and introductions, prayer, meditation, warm-up, choreography, practice, next steps (next practice or upcoming ministry engagement), and closing prayer.

Liturgical Dance Ministry Practice

Step 1. Welcome & Introduction Through prayer the leader (or designee) welcomes the dancers back to the ministry and introduces returning or new dancers.

Step 2. Prayer: Leader (or designee) prays to welcome in the holy spirit and to remove any distractions.

Step 3. Song Meditations: The ministry membership studies the lyrics and meditates on the song to be ministered through dance.

Step 4. Warm-up: Stretching (Yoga) and Dance Technique Review

Step 5. Choreography: Develop dance steps and combinations to the song to be ministered through dance.

Step 6. Next Steps: Announcements, next practice dates, upcoming dance ministry engagements, and information pertinent to the dance ministry.

Step 7. Prayer: Through prayer the leader (or designee) ends the practice. Prays for the ministry and the membership individually and collectively; prays for the church leadership and mission of the church.

Liturgical Dance Ministry Practice

Welcome & Introductions

Opening Prayer

Song Meditation

Warm-up (Stretching)

Choreography

Next Steps: Upcoming Practices, Dance Ministry Engagements and Announcements

Closing Prayer

Chapter VI.

Dancers Called To Worship

Anyone can dance in the church, but only a few are called to minister through dance. **Ephesians 3:7** I was made a minister, according to the gift of God's grace which was given to me according to the working of His power (kjv). This call is identical to the call to preach and share God's word. If you are called to dance, you will have the gift of dance and dance will reside in your heart. The gift of dance does not mean that a dancer will be a professional dancer, the gift of dance means that God will use a dancer in the worship experience and ensure that the dancer has the required skills required to serve his purpose in ministry. Where, God's purpose will vary from dancer to dancer.

In **Acts 1:24** the Bible reads "Lord, you know everyone's heart. Show us which of these two you have chosen" (NIV). Does this mean that everyone that has the talent of dance is called and gifted to dance for God? Does this mean that everyone that dances in church is an expert or highly skilled dancer? Absolutely not, God anoints his disciples in multiple ways. You can have an anointed dancer, who has no legs or limited mobility. You can have an anointed dancer that has never danced. Whereas, on the other hand you can have an experienced dancer that can teach dance on all levels across the nation, but that experienced dancer is not anointed to minister and worship God through dance. God only anoints those that he has chosen to minister and worship through dance; therefore, as written in the Bible, **1 Timothy 4:14** do not neglect the spiritual gift within you, which was bestowed on you.

God always provides. God will ensure that those individuals called to minister through dance, have the gift of dance and skills needed to accommodate the gift of dance. God will anoint each chosen dancer with a specific gift of dance. **Romans 12:6**, the Bible reads "since we have gifts that differ according to the grace given to us, each of us is to exercise them accordingly: if prophecy, according to the proportion of his faith". Gifted dancers will be anointed with a specific skill level that is required to serve God's people in a manner that is pleasing to God. In **Proverbs 18:16** the Bible reads, "your gift will make room for you", suggesting that God will ensure that each dancer has that which is needed to minister through dance for that specific ministry at that given time. In the Bible, **2 Corinthians 6:3** reads "we put no stumbling block in anyone's path, so that our ministry will not be discredited". Dancers chosen or handpicked by God will be placed in a dance ministry with a specific skill level and responsibility. **1 Peter 4:10** As each one has received a special gift, employ it in serving one another as good stewards of the manifold grace of God.

When you look at the dance ministries around the country, it is amazing the diversity and multiple competencies found on dance ministries. **2 Corinthians 9:15** Thanks be to God for his indescribable gift! **Romans 11:29** for the gifts and the calling of God are irrevocable. But what is more amazing is watching how God uses each dancer to minister. Watching how God uses a ministry of new and beginner dancers to minister through dance and the experience is more powerful, than a dance team of professional dancers. Now does this mean that God does not anoint professional dancers, absolutely not. God has anointed those dancers with professional dance skills needed to minister through dance at a different skill level. God uses all dancers with various dance skills to minister and nurture in the Holy Spirit; validating the importance of having the right dancers in the right place at the right time to minister through dance. **1 Corinthians 12:4** Now there are varieties of gifts, but the same Spirit. That is why, it is important that dance ministry leaders and dancers recognize the importance and differences between dancing and ministering.

A successful dance ministry leader must be able to discern the difference between the desire to dance because that is the desire of the flesh or the desire to dance because the dancer was chosen to dance. This is important for dance ministry leaders because the leader must be in constant prayer with God to ensure that each dancer is being used as God has gifted the dancer to be used. The dance minister leader is then challenged with using each dancer in areas of their gifts, in efforts to ensure that Gods people are blessed. **1 Peter 4:11** Whoever speaks, is to do so as one who is speaking the utterances of God; whoever serves is to do so as one who is serving by the strength which God supplies; so that in all things God may be glorified through Jesus Christ, to whom belongs the glory and dominion forever and ever. Amen. (kvj)

Who is Called to Worship?

1. If you believe in your heart that God told you to minister and worship through dance.
2. If you believe that you communicate with God through dance movements.
3 . If you believe that you can share God's word with dance movements.
4. If you have the desire to serve God through dance.
5. If you are committed to the dance ministry.
6. If you are discipline and committed to the dance ministry requirements.
7. If you believe that God has given you the gift of dance.
8. If you are trainable and willing to be trained to be a better dancer for God's use.
9. If you understand the difference between dancing and ministering.
10. If you understand that you are dancing for God and not in competition.

11. If you minister through dance for God's purpose only and give God all the glory.

12. If you have the mental and physical ability to minster through dance.

13. If you respect how dance became a part of the worship experience.

14. If you recognize that you minister through dance for an audience of one, GOD!

15. If you worship to usher in the holy spirit in efforts to save souls.

CHAPTER VII.

Dance Worship Experience

What does the perfect dance ministry worship experience look like? What does it feel like? Well of course there is no one size fit all. Each dance ministry worship experience will be different. Even if the same dancers minister to the same song for the same audience, each time the experience will be different. If you are ministering according to God's will, God will use that experience for what is needed at that time for that audience. This is not measured based on how many people are standing in the congregation or how many people are crying in the congregation, or any other physical factor that shows outward success. The perfect dance worship experience is the experience that touches the individuals that God has targeted for that experience, most often dancers will have no idea. Of course, it is nice to see people enjoying the dance worship experience, but the goal is much larger than anything that man could imagine.

Characteristics of an Anointed Dance Worship Experience:

1. The dancers feel exhausted and filled with the holy spirit.
2. The dancers get lost in the worship experience and let go of choreography.
3. The dancers are ministering as if they are in the room with only God.
4. The dancer's movements are communicating a message to God's people.
5. God's people get lost in the worship experience.
6. The dance ministry experience aligns with the preached word to further elaborate the message from God.
7. God's people physically demonstrate the understanding of God's message presented through the dance (shouting, crying, worshipping, clapping, etc.).
8. The dancers continue worshipping through dance after the song has ended.
9. The congregation transitions into deep worship during or at the conclusion of the song ministered through dance.
10. Someone gives his/her life to Christ as a result of the dance worship experience.
11. People show public interest in joining the dance ministry as a result of the dance worship experience.
12. Feeling the Holy Spirt moving in the atmosphere during and after the dance worship experience.

	Do's (Worship)	Do Not (Dance)
1	Minister through dance as if you are dancing for an audience of one "GOD".	Do not use the dance ministry experience as a competition or self-promotion opportunity.
2	Each dancer is a worshipper, worshipping God through dance.	The dancers are dancing out the practiced choreography.
3	Dancers must be in the mindset of worship, using every movement to honor God.	Dancers focused on the dance steps, choreography, and who's watching.
4	"I'm going to minister".	"I'm going to perform".
5	Use every dancer equally, recognize that each dancer has a purpose on the ministry.	Align the dancers based on dance technique and skill.
6	Let the Holy Spirit guide the ministry.	Highlight or promote only skilled dancers.
7	Pray, meditate, and seek song selections from God.	Dancing to your favorite song.
8	Always have the hair secured and neatly off of the face.	Dancers' hair worn loose and swinging uncontrollably while dancing.
9	Require dancers to wear tights or leggings with every garment.	Dancers dance in leotard and tights.
10	Dancers are only allowed to wear soft skin tone makeup.	Allow the dancers to wear various colored makeup (blues, greens, purples), if the make up is professionally applied.

Song Selection Aligned to Scripture

It is suggested that dance ministry leaders align scripture to the song of choice to minister and seek God for confirmation. Only God knows exactly what he wants to communicate to the people through the dance. God knows the gifts, talents, and influence within the dance ministry better than anyone. God will speak to you and guide you as you meditate with him in His Word. According to **Matthew 7:7-8** (7) Ask, and it shall be given you; seek, and ye. shall find; knock, and it shall be opened unto you. (8) For everyone that asketh, receiveth, and he that seeketh. findeth; and to him that knocketh it shall be opened.

Reflection

(1) What steps do you use to select a song to minister through dance?

_____

_____

_____

_____

_____

(2) As the dance ministry leader, do you select all the songs to minister?
( ) Yes ( ) No

If yes, why?

_____

_____

_____

_____

If no, who and how are songs selected to minister through dance?

_____

_____

_____

_____

(3) Do you believe the song selection is the responsibility of the leader, the dancers, or both? Explain.

_____

_____

_____

_____

_____

The dance ministry leader is responsible for ensuring that all song selections to minister are appropriate. The dance ministry leader must be aware and embrace the mission of the church. But also, the dance ministry leader must be in constant communication and alignment with the church leadership (Pastor, Bishop, Minster, etc.) and the vision and direction of the church. The dance ministry leader must also recognize that the dance ministry is a part of the worship team and a part of the worship experience during service. The dance ministry leader must actively participate in church bible study and spiritual growth to further understand the direction and vision of church. To that note, dance song selections should be made in collaboration with the worship leader to ensure that the dance song selection aligns with the service.

- **Luke 4:8** "It is written: 'Worship the Lord your God and serve him only" (NIV).
- **Luke 4:8** "And Jesus answered and said unto him, get thee behind me, Satan: for it is written, Thou shalt worship the Lord thy God, and him only shalt thou serve" (KJV).

Collectively, all songs included in the worship experience, whether sung by the choir or used to minister through dance must guide the congregation into the presence of God in preparation for the delivery of God's word. This means that worship leaders, "have to think like an artist bringing together different colors on a canvas to create a beautiful picture; or a story-teller narrating a story in a manner that draws the listener into it and brings it to life" (Choosing Songs for Worship: The Definitive Guide). The worship leader serves as the teacher as outlined in **James 3:1**, "Not many of you should become teachers, my fellow believers, because you know that we who teach will be judged more strictly."

How song selections are a aligned with scripture:

1. Attend bible study regularly.
2. Collaborate with church leadership and the worship team.
3. Pray and seek God's guidance.
4. Based on the theme of the church, make a list of words that support the theme.
5. Research the meaning of the words as listed.

6. Use the meanings of the words to identify supporting songs.

7. Pray and seek guidance from God for the song chosen to minister.

8. Research to ensure that the songs are biblically supported, accurate, relevant, with a clear biblical context.

9. Ensure that the message in the song aligns with the Bible (All "Christian" songs are NOT spiritually based).

10. Keep the focus on God throughout the song selection process.

11. Using the song lyrics and research supporting scriptures.

12. Prioritize familiar songs above new songs, but do not dismiss new songs.

13. Assess the song based on the lyrics, melody, instruments, tone, rhythm, and the ability to minister appropriately through dance.

14. Pray and listen to the Holy Spirit.

15. Learn and understand the words of the song.

16. Build an atmosphere that draws people into the message of the song.

17. Select a melody that appeals to the majority of the targeted audience (know your audience).

18. Recognize the skills of the dancers and how easily the lyrics can be transformed and interpreted through dance movement.

19. Seek final approval from God before introducing the song to the dancers.

Reflection

What will you do differently (if anything) as it relates to song selection to minister through dance?

_____

_____

_____

_____

_____

_____

_____

_____

_____

Vision for the Dance

Every dance ministry leader must seek God first for a clear vision of how to minister a song through dance. Gospel songs can present multiple meanings to people-based on the perceptions of the song. But as the dance ministry leader it is your responsibility to ensure that the song ministered through dance tells the story that God wants the dance ministry to present. A vision is explained as something seen in a dream. Visions are commonly known to come from spiritual rituals. Th Bible records that God has given people visions to demonstrate a specific goal or outcome that God wants to reveal. In **Numbers 12:6**, the Bible says, "hear my words: If there is a prophet among you, I the Lord make myself known to him in a vision; I speak with him in a dream." **Acts 16:9**, A vision appeared to Paul in the night: a man of Macedonia was standing there, urging him and saying. Come over to Macedonia and help us (esv).

The same concept applies to ministering through dance. God has an expectation that the dancers will present the message that he wants to convey. Therefore, it is the dance ministry leader's responsibility to seek God for the vision to minister through dance. Once the vision is understood by dance ministry leader, the responsibility is to minister the song to present the vision given by God. Now, the time comes for the dance ministry leader to be creative and utilize God's gifts to present the vision. But, not just limited to choreography but also determining the colors, garments, props, and the role of each dancer. God has placed every dancer on the ministry for a specific purpose. Each dancer is specifically equipped regardless of age and skill level to offer his or her whole body to accomplish God's will through dance. Part of presenting the vision for the song through dance includes knowing each dancer, knowing each dancer's skill sets, and placing each dancer accordingly to communicate God's vision through dance.

(1) Do you seek God for the vision of the song you plan to minister? Explain:

_____

_____

_____

_____

_____

_____

(2) How do you communicate God's vision to the dancers?

_____

_____

_____

_____

The bible also references other examples of vision that can be considered when leading a dance ministry. In the scripture of Daniel 7:13 the Bible reads, I saw in the night visions, and behold, with the clouds of heaven there came one like a son of man, and he came to the Ancient of Days and was presented before him. Acts 18:9 reads, one night the Lord spoke to Paul in a vision. Jeremiah 23:16 Do not listen to the words of the prophets who prophesy to you, filling you with vain hopes. They speak visions of their own minds, not from the mouth of the Lord. In Habakkuk 2:2, the Bible said, write the vision; make it plain on tablets, so he may run who reads it (ESV).

In Acts 2:17, the Bible reads "In the last days it shall be, God declares, that I will pour out my Spirit on all flesh, and your sons and your daughters shall prophesy, and your young men shall see visions, and your old men shall dream. Acts 9:10-12. (10) Now there was a disciple at Damascus named Ananias. The Lord said to him in a vision, "Ananias." And he said, "Here I am, Lord." (11) And the Lord said to him, "Rise and go to the street called straight, and at the house of Judas look for a man of Tarsus named Saul, for behold, he is praying. (12) and he has seen in a vision a man named Ananias come in and lay his hands on him so that he might regain his sight" (esv).

Dance Technique

Dance ministry is not competitive, nor is it based on professional dance techniques and experiences. However, the dance ministry leader should be aware of basic techniques in efforts to ensure safety and precision as appropriate. Defined and precise dance movements are nice and offer a higher level of clarity; however, with ministry and worship it is not a requirement. In ministry a beginner and a professional dancer have equal opportunity to offer an exceptional worship experience because God has a way of using everyone to glorify his name. Any dance ministry leader serious about leading a dance ministry should participate in a technique class to enhance appropriate dance skills, ensure and promote safety, prevent or minimize injury, promote dancer longevity, build strength and flexibility, and the ability to teach precise and refine movements.

Dance techniques are based on fundamental skills and dance movements, from positioning the body correctly during a performance, to executing skills properly in a routine. Proper technique can be implemented in all areas of dance, regardless of the style of dance or the routine choreographed.

(1) Are you a lifelong learner committed to continued dance development?
( ) Yes ( ) No Explain.

_____

_____

_____

_____

_____

(2) Do you participate in a dance technique program or class. Explain.

_____

_____

_____

_____

_____

(3) What are the benefits of participating in a dance technique program?

_____

_____

_____

_____

_____

Often times dancers get entangled with the choreography and forget about technique, form, and precision. In the article, The Ultimate 7 C(s) of Basic Dance Technique (by Miss P) outlines the seven basic dance techniques that can be used in most dance styles, including praise dancing.

1. **Core** - Your core must be engaged with every movement in dance. Your core gives your entire body tone, balance, and presence.

2. **Clean** - Each movement, no matter how fast it is, or small it is, should be clean, and distinct in and of itself.

3. **Continuous** - When you are moving your energy must flow through your body continuously.

4. **Complete** - With all that great energy going through your body, you should feel compelled to complete each movement to its fullest extension, and you should let yourself do it and enjoy how great it feels and looks.

5. **Control** - Control starts in the mind with intention, then translates to the body with tone. Control gives you stability, poise and power because your energy is focused where it needs to be rather than wherever it happens to be.

6. **Calm** - You must nerve look nervous or uncomfortable when dancing, if you are tense, you will make others tense and destroy all enjoyment of the dance.

7. **Connection** - Connection to the music brings musicality, authenticity, and joy to the dance movements.

"Dance is the art of movement and expression!"

~ Author Unknown

Choreography

The dictionary defines choreography as a noun that represents the art of composing, planning, and arranging dance movements, steps, and patterns of dance. Choreography is the art of designing sequences of physical body movements. Choreography is created by a choreographer, the person who creates movement sequence and align to music. Choreography is used in many forms of art, that include but not limited to ballet, mime, opera, theater, line dancing, cheerleading, gymnastics, fashion, skating, marching band, animated art and other. In the performing arts, choreography applies to human movement and form.

In praise dancing choreography is referred to as the process of creating and aligning dance steps and movements to tell a story, normally accompanied by a gospel song. Although, it is not required, many dance ministry leaders choreograph dance movements to the lyrics of a song. Using a dance movement to better demonstrate and emphasize a word or phrase in a song. Every dancer or dance leader does not have the gift of choreography. Many professional dancers do not have the gift or skill to choreograph dances. But those same dancers have the skill set to dance the movements or steps choreographed by someone else. Choreography is a form of art, that requires creativity, skills, and talents that are gifts from God or learned and trained competencies. It also does not mean that a person that cannot choreograph a dance, cannot be a good dance ministry leader. Although, the skill of choreography is definitely required for the ministry, it does not mean that it has to come from dance ministry leader. The ministry may have co-leaders or designated choreographers that have the gift or talent to choreograph dances. Other ministries may use the actual dancers to choreograph the songs to minister through dance, where each dancer has the opportunity to provide input in the choreography for the dance. Either method can be effective as long as the dance ministry is guided and governed by God's word, prayer, and meditation.

Choreography Process

1. Pray and communicate with God.
2. Continuously listen and meditate on the song.
3. Allow the song to dwell in your heart and spirit.
4. Learn the lyrics of the song.
5. Make interpreting the words your first priority.
6. Extensively study the song: its meaning, its purpose, and its effects.
7. Open up to God and allow the spirit to lead.
8. Move to the music "FREESTYLE" without a plan or ideas for the dance.
9. Meditate on what the song is saying to YOU.
10. Think about the message that the artist is trying to communicate.
11. Concentrate on the meaning and purpose of each phrase and each word.
12. Sign language can be used as a basis to create movement.
13. When you are stuck on a word or phrase, think about a synonym for the word(s) or phrase(s) and how to interpret the synonym.
14. Continuously pray and ask God for guidance and direction.
15. Repeat moves and incorporate solo parts when appropriate.
16. Use You Tube and other virtual platforms for ideas and clarification.
17. NEVER copy, replicate, or duplicate someone else's choreography without the choreographer's consent. Whether the dance is copyright or not, it is unethical to copy another artist's dance without permission. It is no different than stealing. The Bible reads, "thou shall not steal" in **Exodus 20:15** (kvj).

Reflection

(1) Who is the primary choreographer for the ministry?_____

(2) What process do you implement to choreograph a dance?

_____

_____

_____

_____

_____

(3) Do you use other dancers to choreograph or assist with choreography? When? How? Explain.

_____

_____

_____

_____

(4) Do you think the ministry benefits from all dancers participating in the choreography process? Explain your answer.

_____

_____

_____

_____

(5) What (if anything) will you do differently when choreographing a song to minister?

_____

_____

_____

_____

CHAPTER VIII.

Dance Ministry Leaders

Ephesians 4:11 So Christ himself gave the apostles, the prophets, the evangelists, the pastors and teachers.

Hebrews 13:7 Remember your leaders, who spoke the word of God to you. Consider the outcome of their way of life and imitate their faith.

Jeremiah 1:5 Before I formed you in the womb I knew you, before you were born, I set you apart; I appointed you as a prophet to the nations.

Psalm 78:72 With upright heart he shepherded them and guided them with his skillful hand.

Acts 20:28 Pay careful attention to yourselves and to all the flock, in which the Holy Spirit has made you overseers, to care for the church of God, which he obtained with his own blood.

James 3:1 Not many of you should become teachers, my brothers, for you know that we who teach will be judged with greater strictness.

Leaders are individuals that serve to provide guidance and direction to others. Leaders cannot be leaders if they do not have followers. Church leaders are the same, individuals that provide guidance to others, with one difference, it happens in the church.

According to Ensor, in All You Need to Know about Church Leadership,

> Church leadership is about serving others in accordance with Christ's interests so that they can see and accomplish God's purpose for them in the world. A church leader needs qualities that influence and morally support the congregation, the volunteers, and others within the community. Such qualities include moral trustworthiness, social aptitude, empathy, pastoral care, and more.

DANCE MINISTRY LEADER COMPETENCIES

1. Understands, studies, and has leadership experience.
2. Understands the theory behind dance in a biblical context.
3. Understands the purpose of dance in ministry and worship.
4. Understands and works well with people.
5. A life-long learner that always strives to enhance and develop self.
6. Knows how to lead and follow.
7. Can identify and appropriately use talent.
8. Attends bible study and church regularly.
9. Tithes and practices good biblical principles.
10. Has a spirit of fundraising and giving.
11. Has the interest and desire to dance in worship.
12. Understands and practices delegating.
13. Is organized and understands planning.
14. Has available time to dedicate to the ministry inside and outside of church.
15. Understands the principles that govern ministry through dance.
    a. Scripture
    b. Technique
    c. Choreography
    d. Colors
    e. Garments
    f. Props

LITURGICAL DANCE MINISTRY LEADER IS:

1. A Leader that is associated with a house of worship.
2. A Leader that tithes and encourages the dancers to tithe.
3. A Leader that understands the difference between a dance ministry and a dance class.
4. A Leader that uses the bible to guide the dance ministry.
5. A Leader that requires regular prayer, meditation, and fasting of self and dancers.
6. A Leader that appropriately leads a group of dancers to minister through dance
7. A Leader that is continuously educating the dancers (spiritually and professionally).
8. A Leader that recognizes and uses all the individual talents on the dance ministry.

9. A Leader that incorporates spiritual growth and awareness as part of the ministry.
10. A Leader that incorporates appropriate safe dance techniques aligned with skill sets.
11. A Leader that encourages dancers to take risk and elevate to the next level in dance.
12. A Leader that is called to dance and is willing to learn from others.
13. A Leader that can choreograph a dance.
14. A Leader that can humble him/herself to seek choreography help from others.
15. A Leader that encourages participation in a structured dance technique program.
16. A Leader that mentors in and outside of the ministry.
17. A Leader that includes fellowships as part of the ministry experience.
18. A Leader that is a life-long learner, continuously developing self.
19. A Leader that is respected as a ministry leader.
20. A Leader that serves as a mentor and establishes a mentor relationship with each dancer.
21. A Leader that can recognize and pray through tragedy and adversity in the ministry.
22. A Leader that can recognize self-weakness and solicit help.
23. A Leader that leads by example and practices biblical principles daily and on social media.
24. A Leader that appropriately represents the dance ministry and the dancers.
25. A Leader that ensures that dancers are appropriately covered when ministering.
26. A Leader that continuously educates the dancers.
27. A Leader that ensures that the dance ministry is respected throughout the church.
28. A Leader that solicits opportunities for the dancers to minister.
29. A Leader that strives for an exceptional worship experience through dance.
30. A Leader that can identify potential leaders, a successor (new leaders).
31. A Leader that grooms potential leaders (successors) to lead the ministry in the future.
32. A Leader that practices informal and or formal successional planning.

Reflection

Who are you? Use the table below, to identify the qualities of a successful dance ministry leader. (1) Give yourself one point for each item that applies to you. (2) Count your points to determine your total score. (3) Using the rubric to rate your responses.

	Category	"Qualities of a Successful Dance Ministry Leader"	Points
1	Fiscal	Tithes 10% of your gross salary.	
2	Fiscal	Encourages dancers to tithe.	
3	Prayer	Ensures that prayer is incorporated, every time the dance ministry comes together.	
4	Prayer	Spends regular time with God, though regular prayer time, meditation, and fasting.	
5	Bible Study	Attends bible study regularly.	
6	Bible Study	Studies the bible and understands how dance is used in scripture (biblical context).	
7	Bible Study	Educates the dancers on how dance is used in the bible.	
8	Bible Study	Ensures that scriptures are aligned with every song used to minister through dance.	
9	Fellowship	Plans and schedules regular fellowships for the dance ministry.	
10	Mentorship	Identifies potential new leaders and begins the grooming process (succession planning).	
11	Mentorship	Learns each dancer's personalities, competencies, and qualities.	
12	Mentorship	Studies mentorship and succession planning.	

13	Mentorship	Solicit and seek guidance from seasoned dance ministry (leaders) mentors for self and other dancers.	
14	Collaborations	Visit other churches and dance ministries.	
15	Collaborations	Connects and collaborates with other dance ministry leaders.	
16	Leadership	Serves as the leader over the dance ministry and takes responsibility for the ministry and ministry activities.	
17	Leadership	Ensures equity across the ministry with all dancers.	
18	Leadership	Ensures that the song choice, garments, and venues are appropriate for ministry through dance.	
19	Leadership	Employs a safety-first practice, to ensure the safety of each dancer.	
20	Fundraising	Research potential appropriate fundraising activities.	
21	Fundraising	Launch appropriate fundraising activities.	
22	Fundraising	Monitors and tracks fundraising dollars.	
23	Meetings	Holds regular meetings with the dancers and parents (when appropriate).	
24	Ministerial Staff	Attends church leadership meetings.	
25	Ministerial Staff	Meets with church leadership and worship leaders regularly.	
26	Professional Development	Attends dance workshops and dance conferences.	
27	Professional Development	Participate in a structured technique class.	

28	Professional Development	Participates in leadership professional development trainings.	
29	Planning	Outlines a strategic plan with goals and objectives for the dance ministry.	
30	Planning	Collaborates with church leadership, church members, church community, and dancers to develop a dance ministry vision, mission, and core values.	
31	Planning	Implement a schedule of review and evaluation of the dance ministry's strategic plan.	
32	Physical Health	Maintains a healthy and balance diet.	
33	Physical Health	Participates in a regular fitness schedule.	
34	Physical Health	Partners and collaborates with a fitness coach.	
35	Dance Rehearsal	Ensures that the dancers pray in and out of ever dance ministry rehearsal.	
36	Dance Rehearsal	Ensures that song selections are appropriate for ministry, aligns with scripture, and supports the vision of church.	
37	Dance Rehearsal	Uses choreography that incorporates appropriate dance movements, recognizing the skill sets of each dancer on the ministry.	
38	Dance Rehearsal	Selects appropriate dance ministry garments for the worship experience.	
39	Dance Rehearsal	Schedules rehearsal days and times that are appropriate for the dance ministry membership.	
40	Dance Rehearsal	Before introducing choreography to the dancers, time is scheduled for meditation, conversation, and understanding of the lyrics.	
		TOTAL POINTS	

What is your score _____ (Count the points and use rubric for a final rating).

Points	Assessment Criteria
1- 8	**UNSATISFACTORY.** You need work. This may NOT be the appropriate time for you to serve as a dance ministry leader.
9 - 16	**FAIR.** Your ministry could benefit from you developing your leadership skills. You need to self-reflect and recognize areas that need improvement. You may want to consider training under a more seasoned leader to develop before attempting to lead a dance ministry.
17 - 24	**GOOD.** You are moving in the right direction, but you still have a way to go. Recognize areas that can be improved and use the tips to develop in those areas.
25 - 32	**VERY GOOD.** You have the qualities of a good dance ministry leader. But recognize the areas that can be improved and use the tips to develop in those areas.
33 - 40	**EXECELLENT.** You have the qualities of an exceptional dance ministry leader. But continue to develop yourself and grow the ministry. Never stop learning.

(1) What areas do you need to develop or improve?

_____

_____

_____

_____

_____

_____

(2) What strategies will you implement to develop in those areas to become a better dance ministry leader?

_____

_____

_____

_____

_____

(3) Who can you connect with to assist you with your development process as a dance ministry leader?

_____

_____

_____

_____

_____

(4) Do you have a mentor? Who? _____

(5) Is there anyone else that can serve as a mentor to help you develop as a dance ministry leader? Who?

_____

_____

_____

_____

_____

(6) How and when will you connect with the potential new mentor(s) and request a mentorship relationship?

_____

_____

_____

_____

_____

CHAPTER IX.

Planning

(1) Do you believe that planning should be deliberate? YES ( ) NO ( )

(2) Do you believe that planning should be documented (written)?
YES ( ) NO ( ).

Why? _____

_____

_____

_____

_____

_____

Prayerfully, your response was "YES" because planning is instrumental to all success. You may not currently have an established documented plan; you may have never even thought that a plan was necessary for the dance ministry. But recognizing that planning is important, is the first and the key step to success. Have you heard the saying, "If you don't plan your future, society will plan it for you!" If you are not planning your own destiny, you will look up in a year, 2 years, 4 years, 5 years, 10 years, and you will be in the same place where you started, showing no or limited growth and development.

The best definition of planning:

Planning is the process of outlining the activities required to achieve a desired goal. Planning is based on foresight, the fundamental capacity for mental time travel. The evolution of forethought, the capacity to think ahead, is considered to have been a prime mover in human evolution (wikipedia.org).

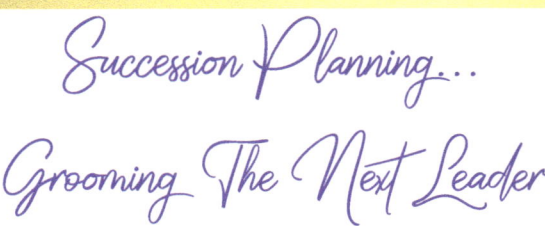

Succession Planning...
Grooming The Next Leader

Henri Fayol was one of the first scholars to recognize human capitol universal organizational needs and championed the use of succession planning. He suggested that leadership replacement planning was a necessity and the only way to avoid organizational failures that resulted from recruiting unprepared individuals to fill key positions. Fayol understood the importance of planning and the need for organizations to invest in its internal personnel through training and professional leadership development programs, which ultimately led to the birth of succession planning (Rothwell, 1994, 2001, 2005).

Historically, succession planning was described as a mechanism to ensure that pools of qualified leaders were available for future leadership vacancies (Levit & Gikakis, 1994). Charan, Drotter, and Noel (2001) defined succession planning as a process of "perpetuating the enterprise by filling the pipeline with high performing people to assure that every leadership level has an abundance of these performers to draw from, both now and in the future" (p. 167). Other scholars viewed succession planning as a strategic process by which an organization ensured the stability of tenured personnel; through the internal identification of candidates to transition into a selected position vacancies (Carroll, 2004; Carter, 1986; Caudron; 1999; Levit & Gikakis, 1994; Rothwell, 1994, 2001, 2005).

The primary objective of succession planning was described as being positioned to get the right person with "the right skills, in the right place, at the right time" to ensure sustainability. Although, succession planning research concentrates on corporate America, the concept also applies to other organizations, education, churches, groups, etc. *In the Trustee's Perceptions of Succession Planning in Maryland Community Colleges* dissertation, Dr. Daphne Snowden concluded that succession planning is not widely used because leaders do not fully understand succession planning and its benefits. More importantly, leaders do not understand the consequences of not having a succession plan in place!

Well, the time is now that leaders become educated and understand the importance of succession planning for growth and continuation of corporate organizations, educational environments, churches, and ministries. William Vanderbloemen explained in *Next: Pastoral Succession That Works*, that the day is quickly approaching for every church leader to recognize that he or she will need to identify a successor to take over. Take a look around, on average most church leaders (pastors and ministry leaders) are 45 years of age and older. It is no secret that the current church leaders will be stepping down or stepping back from leading ministries, either by choice or force. What is the plan? Linda Stanley, Vice President and Team Leader for Leadership Network, revealed that the "NO PLAN" is most common among leadership today.

But how does the "no plan" concept impact churches and ministries. Well let's reflect, how many times have you experienced a church ministry dissolve because the leader left the church, the leader stepped down, the leader got mad, the leader had a baby, the church removed the leader because of an inappropriate action, the leader got married, or for whatever reason but the leader stopped leading the ministry and the ministry died. Well, that is the result of "no plan", if you do not have a plan for something to continue than that is what will happen it will NOT continue because, as the leader you did not plan in advance for its continuation. It is that simple! So, because you are reading this book, you are clearly a leader that wants to change the game…start your planning process today.

How to develop a succession plan for a dance ministry?

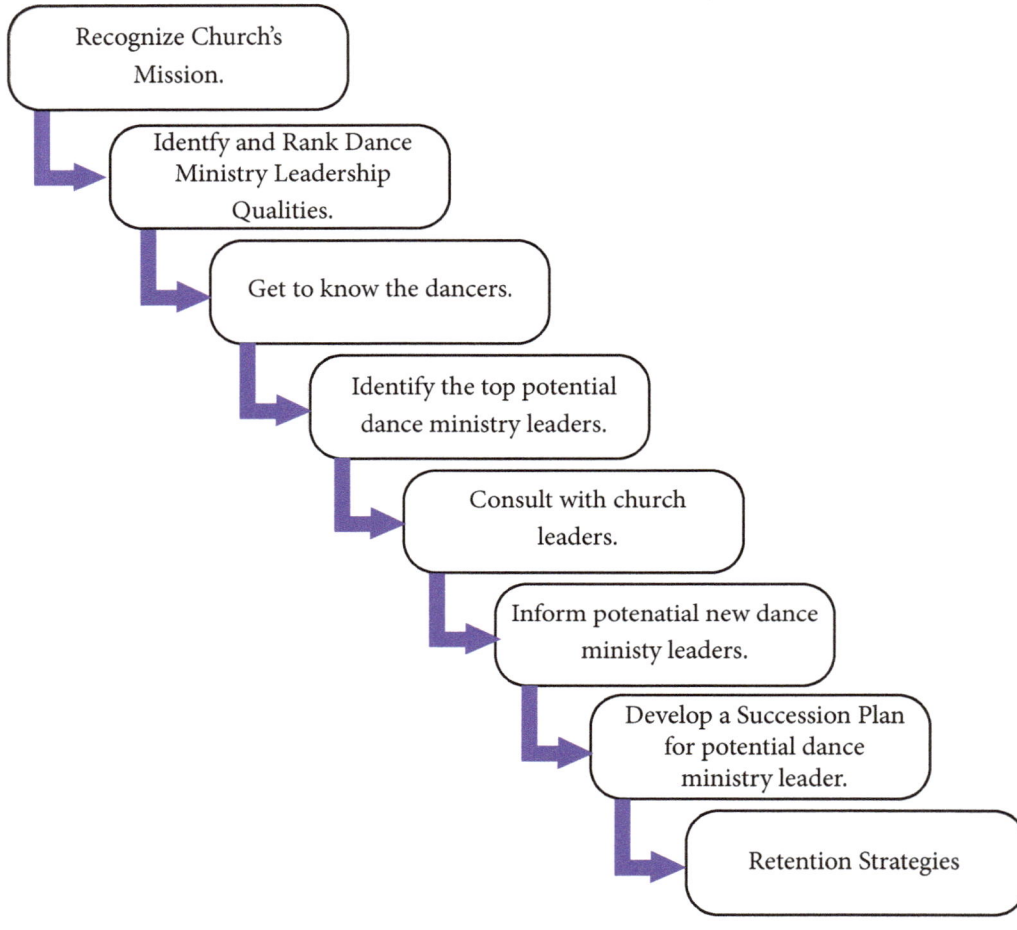

Recognize Church's Mission.

Identfy and Rank Dance Ministry Leadership Qualities.

Get to know the dancers.

Identify the top potential dance ministry leaders.

Consult with church leaders.

Inform potenatial new dance ministy leaders.

Develop a Succession Plan for potential dance ministry leader.

Retention Strategies

STEP-BY-STEP PROCESS

1. Learn the Church's mission and future plans.
2. Identify the qualities and competencies needed to be a successful leader of the dance ministry and create an inventory list of those competencies.
3. Rank and prioritize the inventory of competencies.
      a. Examples of potential qualities and competencies needed in a NEW dance ministry leader. (Note: This list is not exhaustive, just a few examples).
           i. Bible Training

  ii. Choreography Dance Training

  iii. Leadership Training

  iv. Trained Mentor

  v. Fundraising

  vi. Event Planning

4. Get to know your dancers (collect data on each dancer and analyze):

  a. Learn their spiritual upbringing and development.

  b. Learn about their professional careers.

  c. Learn their educational background.

  d. What are their aspirations?

  e. What are their ministry goals?

  f. What are their dancer goals?

  g. Do they have the potential and want to lead the dance ministry?

5. Identify the top three to five potential leaders within the dance ministry.

6. Evaluate each dancer's potential to lead (know his or her pros and cons).

7. Rank the potential leaders from (1-5), with one being the top potential incoming dance ministry leader "successor".

8. Inform the church leaders of your observation for the next dance ministry leader (successor) and seek advice from leadership.

9. Inform the dancer that he/she has been recognized as a potential leader for the dance ministry (the successor).

10. Develop a succession plan for the potential next dance ministry leader.

11. Implement retention strategies to ensure that leadership qualities are maintained and further developed until leadership is transferred to the new leader.

*Note: succession plans will vary based on dancers' current competencies and needed competencies to lead the dance ministry.

Retention Strategy Examples (might include):

  a. Permit the successor to lead the dance ministry in the absence of the current leader.

  b. Allow the successor to serve as a co-leader of the dance ministry with the current dance ministry leader.

  c. Participate in leadership development programs.

  d. Attend dance ministry workshops and conferences.

  e. Transfer responsibilities to the potential dance ministry successor.

Note: The list will vary from dance ministry to dance ministry, based on the characteristics of the church, the dancers, leadership, and the community of potential new dancers.

Have you positioned yourself to **Pass the Baton** to a willing, trained, well-equipped potential dancer to lead the dance ministry in your absence?

If you can answer **YES**. You are an exceptional, confident leader on your way to greatness. Explain, how you have prepared to "Pass the Baton" to the next potential dance ministry leader.

_____

_____

_____

_____

_____

_____

_____

_____

_____

_____

_____

_____

_____

_____

_____

If you answered NO, here is your chance. Examine your current dancers and identify the dancers that are most prepared to be groomed to grab the baton and continue the dance ministry to honor the current dancer ministry leader's legacy. Please do not be so arrogant to believe that there are no dancers ready to be groomed for the leadership role in your absence because if that is the case then you as a leader need more leadership development in leading a dance ministry. This does not mean that your successor is ready today to lead the dance ministry, but that the successor has the potential, ability, and willingness to be trained and groomed to serve as your successor and lead the dance ministry in the future.

List the name(s) of the top five dancers that you have chosen to groom for the dance ministry leadership role in your absence. Rank the dancers, number 1 should be the co-leader or the dancer that you currently leave in charge in your absence. Also, explain WHY the dancers were selected. In Exodus 18:21 the Bible reads, "select capable men from all the people—men who fear God, trustworthy men who hate dishonest gain and appoint them as officials over thousands, hundreds, fifties and tens". (kjv)

Dance Ministry "Successor"

	Dancer (Name)	Why was this dancer selected (be specific and detailed)?
1		
2		
3		
4		
5		

(1) What is your plan for training the identified potential new dance ministry leaders?

_____

_____

_____

_____

_____

(2) How will you carefully implement this process without offending or insulting other dancers?

_____

_____

_____

_____

(3)Who will you partner (other leaders) with to assist you with this process and why?

_____

_____

_____

_____

_____

I will instruct you and teach you in the way you should go;
I will counsel you with my loving eye on you.
-Psalm 32:8

Five-Year Strategic Plan

What is the best definition of planning?

Planning is the process of outlining the activities required to achieve a desired goal. Planning is based on foresight. The evolution of forethought, the capacity to think ahead, is considered to have been a prime mover in human evolution (wikipedia.org).

What is the best definition of strategic planning?

Strategic planning is a process used in the corporate sector to establish a pathway to accomplish the agency mission and vision. The strategic planning process Is used to establish a long-term plan that includes mission, vision, core values, and goals. The plan outlines how to accomplish its goals and when to expect to successfully accomplish the goals. The strategic planning process recognizes the organization's current state and ideally where the organization would like to be by a designated completion date. Specifically, the strategic planning process is deliberate and used to establish a clear pathway to success. There are no limits for the strategic planning process but in the business world strategic planning refers to a five-year plan.

Planning is the process of summarizing the roadmap to the future. The planning process outlines the big picture goal and milestones or small steps that lead to the success of the big picture outcome. The planning process outlines where you intend to be by the end of a designated timeframe. Planning is one of the most important activities that companies do regularly to provide an opportunity to set the overall direction for the company through goals, objectives, budgets, and performance measures. Planning is a necessity for the success of everything, whether it is planning the future of a multi-million-dollar company, a small corner store, a school, a church, or a church ministry. Therefore, the praise dance ministry is not exempt from the planning process and the ministry must plan to ensure ministry success.

Examples of dance ministry goals that can be included in a strategic plan:
1. The dance ministry will raise $10,000 from fundraising by December 31, 2027 to support the dance ministry expenses and to offer donations to the church.

2. The dance ministry will increase dance membership by 10% annually representing a 50% membership increase in the next five years.
3. The dance ministry will develop a training plan manual to ensure that dancers understand the biblical scripture context for dance in the worship experience by December 2025.

Reflection

Do you have a Strategic Plan for the Dance Ministry: YES ( ) or NO ( )

If "YES" use this opportunity to review, revise and update (where applicable) the strategic plan. If "NO" now is the perfect opportunity to establish a vision, mission, and core values for the dance ministry accompanied by goals and objectives to ensure future success. Now, please do not try to accomplish this in a silo, this is a strategic plan that includes all vested constituents: Bishop, Pastor, ministers, worship leaders, dancers, parents, and church community representation. As the dance ministry leader, it is the leader's responsibility to facilitate the planning process, capture, and document internal and external feedback throughout the planning process. Let's get started! What is the name of the dance ministry? What is the mission, vision, and core values for the ministry?

DANCE MINISTRY: _____

Mission

A mission is a formal synopsis of the direction and principles of a company, group, organization, or individual.

The mission for _____ Dance Ministry is

_____

_____

_____

_____

_____

_____

Vision

A vision is the imagined future of the company, organization, group, or individual that does not currently exist.

The vision for the _____ Dance Ministry is

_____

_____

_____

_____

_____

_____

Core Values

Core values are the fundamental beliefs used as the guiding principles to manage human behavior and to understand the distinction between right and wrong.

Core Value (Examples): Prayer, Ministry, Worship, Honesty, Integrity, Leadership, Precision, Ethical, Caring, Fellowship, Spiritual Growth, Teaching, Learning, and Self-Development.

Ministry Title: _____

The Core Values for the dance ministry are:

1. _____

2. _____

3. _____

4. _____

5. _____

Goals

A goal is a desire to reach a designated outcome, that includes the intention, intent, purpose, design, aim, or objectives to accomplish success.

Do you currently have goals for the dance ministry? Yes (   ) No (   )

1. If you answered "YES", what are those goals?

a. _____

_____

_____

b. _____

_____

_____

c. _____

_____

_____

d. _____

_____

_____

2. If you answered No, it is not to late. Let's get started, the process starts here and now. Below you will find an example of an annual goal with objectives, using a SMART goal format for a dance ministry.

Smart Goals

Planning is important for the dance ministry or any ministry. Planning is one of the most important leadership techniques required for success. A plan can be long term or short term, but you must have a plan. The plan is the road map to success and the goals are the driving force. When writing a strategic plan, SMART goals are recommended.

SMART GOALS are goals that are **S**pecific, **M**easurable, **A**ttainable, **R**ealistic and **T**imely.

- **SPECIFIC** meaning the goals must be written in a precise and detailed manner that eliminates confusion, misunderstandings, and uncertainty.
- **MEASURABLE** meaning the goals must be quantifiable, measurable, and provide a clear rubric to assess accomplishments.
- **ATTAINABLE** meaning the goals must be reasonably achievable.
- **REALISTIC** meaning the goals must be something that makes sense and can be achieved under normal circumstances.
- **TIMELY** meaning the goals must be met in a preset time frame.

An example of a Strategic Plan (Five-Year Goal): In the next five years the Faith-Faith Dance Ministry (for all ages) will be divided into five separate dance ministries, separated by age to create individual age-appropriate dance ministries by December 31, 2028.

> (a) Youth Dance Ministry (ages 3 - 12) December 2024.
> (b) Teen Dance Ministry (ages 13 - 19) December 2025.
> (c) Young Adults Dance Ministry (ages 20 - 30) December 2026.
> (d) Adult Dance Ministry (ages 31- 55) December 2027.
> (e) Seniors Dance Ministry (ages 56 – Up) December 2028.

BREAKDOWN:

- **SPECIFIC** outlines how the age groups will be separated.
- **MEASURABLE** there will be five separate dance ministries by December 31, 2027.
- **ATTAINABLE** five years is reasonable, you can separate out one age group each year.
- **REALISTIC** to identify and train new leaders for each age group.
- **TIMELY** the goal will be successfully achieved in five years by December 31, 2027.

What do you want the dance ministry to achieve in the next five years? Be creative and aim high. Create a plan to take the ministry to the next level. Do not focus on the how, why, or cost? *DREAM BIG!*

Steps For Writing Smart Goals

STEP I   List what you want to accomplish for the dance ministry.

STEP II   Seek deliberate guidance from church leadership and the community.

STEP III   Meet with the worship leader to discuss your thoughts and seek input?

STEP IV   Solicit input from the dancers and their parents (where appropriate).

STEP V   Categorize your thoughts in specific categories. (Examples: spiritual growth, fundraising, membership, professional development training, and leadership).

STEP VI   Write a specific SMART goal for each category of concern.

STEP VII   Write annual, quarterly, monthly, and weekly objectives to accomplish each strategic plan goal.

STEP VIII   Share the goals and objectives with church leadership, dancers, and the community.

STEP IX   Document a plan and timeline for implementation.

STEP X   Create a schedule of review and revision for all goals and objectives.

Five-Year Strategic Goal I

_____

_____

_____

Five-Year Strategic Goal II

_____

_____

_____

Five-Year Strategic Goal III

_____

_____

_____

Five-Year Strategic Goal IV

_____

_____

_____

Five-Year Strategic Goal V

_____

_____

_____

"Paint your dreams through the art of dance!"

~ drs

Annual Goals and Objectives

The annual goals and objectives are the annual (12 month) goals used to reach the five-year strategic goals as outlined in the Five-Year Strategic Plan. The annual goals must be directly aligned to a five-year strategic plan goal, and the strategic plan goals are aligned to the mission and vision for the dance ministry. The dance ministry mission must be aligned with the church mission

Many leaders ask how many goals are necessary for success?

There is no magic number that tells how many goals to have. The *RULE OF THUMB* is to have: (1) a goal to develop the dancers individually, (2) a goal to develop the ministry as a whole, (3) a goal to recruit new dancers, (4) a goal to address the dance ministry's impact in the worship experience and (5) a goal to raise funding for the ministry. But also create goals that do not pigeon hole or minimize the ministry.

Annual Goal (EXAMPLE): Prayer, fasting, and meditation will be embedded protocol when approaching a new song to minister by December 31, 20XX.

1) Objective (1): Prayer, fasting, and mediation will be introduced to the ministry by January 31, 20XX (1 month).

2) Objective (2): Dancers are required to research and report why prayer, fasting, and mediation are critical to the dance ministry experience by February 28, 20XX (2 months).

3) Objective (3): The dance ministry leader will plan a work shop to educate and collaborate with dancers about prayer, fasting and meditation in April 20XX (4 months).

4) Objective (4): The dance ministry leader will lead the dance ministry in prayer, fasting, and meditation for three months (January, February, and March) and then create a schedule (effective June 1, 20XX) that re quires all members to lead the process on a monthly rotation (6 months).

Mininstry Name: _____

Annual Goal I

_____

_____

_____

Objectives

1. _____

_____

_____

2. _____

_____

_____

3. _____

_____

_____

4. _____

_____

_____

5. _____

_____

_____

Annual Goal II

_____

_____

_____

Objectives

1. _____

_____

_____

2. _____

_____

_____

3. _____

_____

_____

4. _____

_____

_____

5. _____

_____

_____

Annual Goal III

_____

_____

_____

Objectives

1. _____

_____

_____

2. _____

_____

_____

3. _____

_____

_____

4. _____

_____

_____

5. _____

_____

_____

Annual Goal IV

_____

_____

_____

Objectives

1. _____

_____

_____

2. _____

_____

_____

3. _____

_____

_____

4. _____

_____

_____

5. _____

_____

_____

"Share your soul with the world through dance!"

Chapter X.

Gospel Physical Fitness

Physical Fitness is the process or framework used to becoming a healthy human-being. *Physical* refers to the bodily condition aligned with the mental and emotional state of the human being. *Fitness* refers to the bodily conditions and the body being readily able to carry out daily tasks, without yielding to fatigue and lack of energy. Together, physical fitness refers to a regular physical movement regiment used to promote strong muscles and toning. Physical fitness is used to improve and eliminate respiratory and cardiovascular health problems. Also, to enhance overall health and well-being of others. Regular physical fitness routines have shown to be effective in maintaining good health, height and weight balance, and with the reduction of health risk factors. Conditions that may include (but not limited to) diabetes, heart condition, lupus, autoimmune deficiency, lung disease, thyroid dysfunction, kidney disease, hypertension, HIV, asthma, and cancers.

What is Gospel Fitness?

Gospel fitness refers to fitness in the same manner as physical fitness. The distinct difference is the "Gospel" portion. Gospel Fitness is the process or framework used to becoming a healthy well-being, mentally, physically, and spiritually. It is an opportunity for like mind individuals to come together to fellowship through prayer, scripture reading, and physical workout.

In **1 Timothy 4:8** the bible reads, "for bodily exercise profiteth little: but godliness is profitable unto all things, having promise of the life that now is, and of that which is to come". In **1 Corinthians 6:19-20**, the bible reads, (19) What? know ye not that your body is the temple of the Holy Ghost which is in you, which ye have of God, and ye are not your own? (20) For ye are bought with a price: therefore, glorify God in your body, and in your spirit, which are God's. **1 Corinthians 9:24**, "Do you not know that in a race all the runners run, but only one receives the prize? So run that you may obtain it". Lastly, **1 Corinthians 10:31** "so, whether you eat or drink, or whatever you do, do all to the glory of God". (ESV) **Isaiah 40:31** But those who wait on the Lord shall renew their strength. They shall mount up with wings like eagles, they shall run and not be weary, they shall walk and not faint." (NKJV).

What are the benefits of Gospel Fitness?

1. Provides an opportunity to fellowship outside the church.
2. Provides an opportunity to fellowship with a physical fitness goal.
3. Provides an opportunity to study and understand bible scriptures.
4. Provides an opportunity to pray with like mind individuals.
5. Provides an opportunity to request prayer for self and others.
6. Provides an opportunity to establish a prayer circle of individuals of like commonalities.
7. Provides an opportunity to listen to good gospel music.
8. Provides an opportunity to meditate on gospel music.
9. Provides an opportunity to recognize God's goodness.
10. Provides an opportunity to share God's goodness with others.
11. Provides an opportunity to be thankful and grateful.
12. Provides an opportunity to develop the human body through a structured fitness routine.
13. Holds individuals accountable to a structured fitness program.
14. Provides a program that supports mental and physical development.
15. Provides a program that will assist with common health disorders.
16. Provides a program that enhances physical appearance.
17. Provides a program that improves self-esteem.
18. Provides a program that can assist with physical rehabilitation goals.
19. Provides a program that is suitable for all ages.
20. Provides a program for family fellowship with a purpose.
21. Provides a program that supports healthy living.

Gospel Fitness Routine

1. **Opening Prayer**
2. **Bible Scripture Reading**
3. **Warm-Up:** Yoga stretching routine to a gospel song
4. **Gospel Physical Fitness Routine:** A mixed physical fitness routine accompanied by gospel music:

      a. Aerobics

      b. Kick-Boxing

      c. Weights

      d. Zumba

      e. Yoga

      f. Cardiovascular Exercise

5. **Cool-Down:** A routine to Gospel music that decreases the breathing patterns and heart rate.
6. **Closing Prayer**

NOTE: Throughout the routine the instructor incorporates spiritual and scripture messages to encourage the Saints to continue and push through the pain. In **Philippians 4:13**, the Bible reads "I can do all things through Christ who strengthens me" (kjv).

Reflection

What are three benefits of a gospel physical fitness routine?

_____

_____

_____

_____

_____

_____

Chapter XI.
Virtual Dance Platforms

COVID has forced the world to transition from a face-to-face platform to a virtual platform in many areas and that includes the art of dance. This transition was a not barrier for everyone. For some it was a natural process, but for many others it has been challenging, scary, and overwhelming. Many dancers and leaders have experienced anxiety with dancing in a virtual platform. Some dancers and leaders have stopped dancing because of their discomfort with the virtual platform. This transition has required dance leaders to create a comfortable virtual dance studio, in the home, in the church, etc. In many cases, dance leaders and dancers had to transition bedrooms, living rooms, storage rooms, closets, garages, and basements into virtual dance studios for practice and performances. Further, the virtual platform impacts the audience's experience and ability to connect with the dance experience.

How to create a virtual studio or virtual dance space?

1) Identify a room that is large enough (spacious) to accommodate dance movements.
2) Clean the room and remove anything that may be a distraction to the dance process. An open space helps students to stay focused and the audience to focus on the dance not the virtual studio or virtual room.
3) Permanently or temporarily remove any furniture (tables, chairs, couches, lamps, artwork, flowers, plants, beds, dressers, and appliances).
4) Remove and limit visibility access to pets, children, and other family members.
5) Position the studio to ensure that the background is plain with limited distractions.
6) You may need to create or invest in an appropriate backdrop.

Lighting in the Virtual Platforms

7) Ensure that the virtual studio has good lighting.
8) Use natural lighting (when possible) by placing the back of the camera to the window.
9) Always allow natural lighting to shine on the dancers, eliminating shadows.
10) Eliminate lights shining directly into the camera, hindering visibility.
11) Position light source directly behind the camera and shine the lights in the direction of the area to be filmed or danced.
12) Position dancers to be directly in the spot lighted area of the virtual platform.

Audio and Sound in the Virtual Platform

13) Identify the music source (computer, mobile phones, mp3, Ipod, etc).
14) It is recommended to use internal speakers and bluetooth mobile devices.
15) Place external speakers close to the computer source used for the virtual platform.

Zoom Etiquette

16) Download the Zoom App onto the mobile device or computer.
17) Allow students 15-30 minutes to log-on prior to the start of class, to setup (when appropriate).
18) Click "New Meeting" from the Home Page.
19) Key in Zoom identification number and password.
20) Allow the dancers to enter the virtual Zoom room.
21) Mute all students upon entry.

NOTE: In the beginning phases of creating a virtual platform and with new members, incorporate time before class to assist with individual zoom logon and room setup to ensure that all dancers are comfortable when the class starts.

Chapter XII.

Final Reflections

How has this journal changed your mindset about dance ministries and ministry leadership?

_____

_____

_____

_____

_____

_____

_____

_____

_____

_____

_____

_____

_____

_____

_____

_____

_____

_____

_____

_____

NOTES

NOTES

NOTES

NOTES

References

Adams, Stephanie Butler. My body is the temple: Encounters and revelation of sacred dance and artistry. Fairfax, VA: Xulon Press, 2002.

Bedinghaus, Treva. (May 08, 2019). Liturgical dance as a form of worship: Combining sacred movement with worship. https://www.liveabout.com/praise-dance-basics-1007388

Bellows and Perry, 2005. Graduate mentoring guidebook. https://www.unl.edu/mentoring/why-mentoring-important

Bible. English Standard Version. https://www.biblegateway.com/passage/?search=Genesis%201&version=ESV

Bible. King James Version. https://www.kingjamesbibleonline.org/

Bible. New International Version. https://www.biblegateway.com/passage/?-search=Genesis%201&version=NIV

Bible. New King James Version. https://ebible.com/nkjv/genesis

Carroll, C. (2004). Succession planning: Developing leaders for the future of the organization. [Abstract]. Leadership Abstract, 17, 2.

Chandrasekaran, K. (July, 2020). What does practice mean in dance. https://www.thehindu. com/entertainment/dance/what-does-practice-mean-in-dance/article32034003.ece

Enenche, P. (May 2, 2017). The Significance of spiritual garment ~ Pastor Paul Enenche. http://Gospelhotspot.net

Harris, P.H. Praise and worship with flags: Waging spiritual warfare in the church and home. Bloomington, IN: West Bow Press, 2011.

"History of the sacred dance guild." Online: http://www.sacreddanceguild.org/ (accessed March 20, 2013).

Judy, G. and Bernie. R. Our next chapter: Community colleges and the aging baby boomers. Reprinted from: League of Innovations Leadership. Abstracts. November 2004, Volume 17, Number 11.

Kristine, E. All you need to know about church leadership. A Comprehensive Guide. July 21, 2022. https://donorbox.org/nonprofit-blog/church-leadership#1
Lefevere, P. Dancers' ministry. National Catholic Reporter. Kansas City: Sep 17, 2004.

Lifelong, L. https://www.valamis.com/hub/lifelong-learning#what-is-life-long-learning

Mary, J.J. June, 2019. Why you need a dance mentor. https://blog.joandjax.com/why-you-need-a-dance-mentor-and-how-to-find-one/

Mauro, L. Dancing on higher ground. Dance teacher. New York: Nov 2003.

Maxille, H. "James Cleveland." Encyclopedia of African American music. Vol. 1: A–G, Emmett Price, Tammy L. Kernodle, and Horace Maxille, Jr., eds. (Santa Barbara, CA: Greenwood Press, 2011), 208.

Miss, P., The ultimate 7 'C's of basic dance technique. Tuesday, November 24, 2020. Volume 16924.

Nowik, O. February 17, 2020. 12 Powerful habits of a lifelong learner. Oskar is a blogger and the author of "Brightening: The Positive Attitude That Will Change Your Life" http://www.theafricanamericanlectionary.org/PopupCulturalAid.asp?LRID=426

Richard, J. The Praise dance Life. Ten steps to powerful dance ministry in 2010. https://www.thepraisedancelife.com/10-steps-to-powerful-dance-ministry/page/2/

Rothwell, W. J. (1994). Effective succession planning: Ensuring leadership continuity and building talent from within. New York: Amacon.

Rothwell, W. J. (2001). Effective succession planning: Ensuring leadership continuity and building talent from within (2nd ed.). New York: Amacon.

Rothwell, W. J. (2005). Effective succession planning: Ensuring leadership continuity and building talent from within (3rd ed.). New York: Amacon.

Schmoyer, J. Fasting and spiritual warfare. August 31, 2020. https://www.christiantrainingonline.org/fasting-and-spiritual-warfare/?rmatt=tsid:|cid:1698684404|agid:74739487908|tid:dsa-406202612562|crid:330172770952|nw:g|rnd:10872027351218871933|dvc:c|adp:|loc:9007899&gclid=Cj0KCQjw59n-8BRD2ARIsAAmgPmLWI0rzqRfDmP1Ecv1GZdZB72D0tdBovo9ecaDskRdntey-If6pKA5caAoFqEALw_wcB

An examination of Maryland Community college trustees intentions to promote succession planning. -Morgan State Universit.-ProQuest Dissert Publishing-3516888

Warren Bird. How pastors are passing the leadership baton. Succession plans can destroy a church. Or help it thrive for years to come. What are the keys to success? November 18, 2014

Bible Verses about the Gifts of God. https://bible.knowing-jesus.com/topics/The-Gifts-Of-God

Does the Bible say anything about miming? https://www.gotquestions.org/mime-miming.html

Governing principles. The Law Insider. https://www.lawinsider.com/dictionary/governing-principles

Planning. https://en.wikipedia.org/wiki/Planning

The power of mentorship. The First Tea Blog. https://firsttee.org/category/blog/coaches/mentors/

What does the Bible say about dancing? https://www.gotquestions.org/Christian-dance.html

Interested in Writing and or Publishing your own Book or Journal?
Visit www.a2zbookspublishing.net